This Happy Breed

A Play in Three Acts

Noël Coward

D1382406

Samuel French - London
New York - Toronto - Hollywood

©, Acting Edition, 1945 BY NOEL COWARD
© IN RENEWAL 1973 BY NOEL COWARD

THEATRE ROYAL, HAYMARKET

H. M. TENNENT LTD., in association with JOHN C. WILSON,

present

NOEL COWARD

IN HIS OWN PLAY

THIS HAPPY BREED

Characters in the order of their appearance :

MRS. FLINT (FRANK'S Mother-in-law)	. . .	*Gwen Floyd.*
ETHEL (his Wife)		*Judy Campbell.*
SYLVIA (his Sister)		*Joyce Carey.*
FRANK GIBBONS		*Noel Coward.*
BOB MITCHELL		*Gerald Case.*
REG ⎫		⎧ *Billy Thatcher.*
QUEENIE ⎬(FRANK'S Children)		⎨ *Jennifer Gray.*
VI ⎭		⎩ *Molly Johnson.*
SAM LEADBITTER		*Dennis Price.*
PHYLLIS BLAKE		*Meg Titheradge.*
EDIE (a Maid)		*Beryl Measor.*
BILLY		*James Donald.*

Play directed by THE AUTHOR.   Décor by G. E. CALTHROP.

SYNOPSIS OF SCENES

The Action of the Play passes in the dining-room of the Gibbons's House, No. 17 Sycamore Road, Clapham Common.

ACT I

SCENE 1.—June, 1919.
SCENE 2.—December, 1925.
SCENE 3.—May, 1926.

ACT II

SCENE 1.—October, 1931.
SCENE 2.—November, 1931.
SCENE 3.—May, 1932.

ACT III

SCENE 1.—December, 1936.
SCENE 2.—September, 1938.
SCENE 3.—June, 1939.

THIS HAPPY BREED

ACT I

Scene 1

Time.—*June, 1919.*

Scene.—*The dining-room of Number 17 Sycamore Road, Clapham Common.*

(See the Ground Plan at the end of the book).

On the L. *there is a fireplace. At the back a french window opening on to a narrow stretch of garden. On the* R., *down stage, is the door leading into the hall and through which, when open, the staircase can be seen.*

The time is about eight-thirty in the evening, and, being June, it is still daylight. The french window is open and over the fence at the end of the garden can be seen a may-tree in blossom.

The Gibbons family have only just moved in and so the room is chaotic. There are pale squares on the wallpaper where the last tenant's pictures hung ; a huddle of odd furniture ; several packing-cases and odd parcels, etc., as illustrated. The only piece of furniture in position is a large sideboard which is against the wall on the R., *above the door.*

Mrs. Flint *is sitting in an old-fashioned armchair by the empty fireplace. She is a woman of sixty, soberly dressed in black. She has worn her best clothes for the move as she didn't fancy packing them.* Ethel, *her daughter, a tall woman of thirty-four, is bustling about arranging furniture and undoing parcels. She looks rather hot and untidy as it has been a tiring day. From upstairs comes the sound of intermittent hammering.* Ethel *is carrying a biscuit barrel and a tobacco-jar from the crate* R.C., *to the sideboard* R.

Mrs. Flint (*querulously, glancing up at the ceiling*). What is Frank doing ?

Ethel (*coming down to the crate* R.C.). Putting up the curtains in the front bedroom.

Mrs. Flint. He'll have the house down in a minute.

Ethel (*removing packing paper from the crate*). They've got to be up before we go to bed to-night ; we can't have the whole neighbourhood watching us undress, can we ?

Mrs. Flint. They couldn't see right across the road.

Ethel. Well, they've got to go up some time.

Mrs. Flint. Nobody's thought to put any up in my room, there's no blind either. I suppose I don't matter.

ETHEL (*straightening up, facing* MRS. FLINT). Oh, do shut up grumbling, Mother. You know perfectly well the blinds haven't come yet and your room is at the back, anyhow.

MRS. FLINT. A nice thing if Mr. What's-'is-name next door 'appens to go out into the garden and looks up.

ETHEL (*amused*). We'll send him a note asking him to keep his head down. (*Carrying the paper up* R., *putting it on a box.*)

MRS. FLINT. It's all very fine to laugh.

ETHEL (*coming back to above the crate* C.). I don't know what is the matter with you to-day, Mother, really I don't. Moving in's no picnic anyhow and it only makes things worse to keep complaining all the time. (*She turns to the crate* R.C.)

MRS. FLINT. Me complain? I like that, I must say. I've 'ad a splitting headache ever since two o'clock and I 'aven't so much as mentioned it—rushing about here, there and everywhere, and a fat lot of thanks I get.

ETHEL (*unwrapping an ornament*). It's all right, Mother, cheer up, you'll feel better when you've 'ad a nice cup of tea.

MRS. FLINT. If I ever *do* 'ave a nice cup of tea.

ETHEL (*putting the ornament on the crate* C.). Well, the kettle's on, but Sylvia isn't back yet. (*She returns to the* R.C. *crate.*)

MRS. FLINT (*contemptuously*). Sylvia!

ETHEL (*putting a vase on the crate* C.). She 'ad to go to the U.K. Stores, you know, and that's quite a way.

(*During the next speech* ETHEL *takes out an aspidistra pot and puts the plant in it.*)

MRS. FLINT. She wouldn't 'ave 'ad to do that if she 'adn't forgotten half the things we told her to order. That girl's getting sillier and sillier every breath she takes. I wouldn't be surprised if she 'adn't forgotten the number of the house and lost herself— her and her anæmia!

ETHEL (*going up to the sideboard* R., *with the stand and aspidistra*). Well, she can't help her anæmia, can she, now? (*She returns to the crate* C.)

MRS. FLINT. I don't know how you and Frank put up with her, and that's a fact.

ETHEL (*crossing to the mantel with the vase and ornament*). Now you know as well as I do, Mother, I couldn't let my own sister-in-law live all by herself, could I? Specially after all she's been through.

MRS. FLINT. All she's been through, indeed.

ETHEL (*turning at the fireplace*). I suppose you'll be saying next that she wasn't engaged to Bertie and he wasn't killed, and they've lived 'appy ever after! (*She arranges ornaments.*)

MRS. FLINT. Sylvia 'asn't been through no more than anyone else has, not so much if the truth were known. What she needs is a job of work.

ETHEL (*returning to* C.). She couldn't stand it, she's too delicate, you know what the doctor said.

MRS. FLINT. That doctor'd say anything. Look how he went on over Queenie's whooping-cough, frightening us all to death.

ETHEL. Give us a hand with this little bookcase. We can move it to this corner for the time being, it's not heavy!

MRS. FLINT (*rising reluctantly and helping with the bookcase*). I'm not supposed to lift anything at all, you know—not anything. (*As they carry the bookcase down* L.)

ETHEL. It won't kill you,—all right, all right, don't rush it.

(*They set it down* L.)

Now you can 'ave a nice sit down again.

(MRS. FLINT *returns to* L.C., ETHEL *to the crate* C.)

MRS. FLINT (*sitting again*). This house smells a bit damp to me. I 'ope it isn't.

(ETHEL *takes an ornament from the crate* R.C. *to the crate* C.)

ETHEL. I don't see why it should be, it's not near any water. (*She returns to the* R.C. *crate.*)

MRS. FLINT. Well, you never know. Mrs. Willcox moved into that house in Leatherhead and before she'd been in it for three months she was in bed with rheumatic fever.

(*The front door bell rings.*)

ETHEL (*going to the bookcase down* L., *with ornaments*). That's right, dear, look on the bright side. (*She returns to* C.)

MRS. FLINT. Isn't that the front door?

ETHEL. Yes. (*Unwrapping a clock and taking it to the sideboard* R.) I gave Sylvia a key, she's probably lost it.

MRS. FLINT. Perhaps she's been run over, and it's the police come to tell us.

(ETHEL *goes into the hall. After a moment* SYLVIA *enters. She is a pale woman of thirty-four, carrying a large parcel of groceries which she plumps down on the sideboard with a sigh and then comes down* R.C. ETHEL *then enters and goes to the sideboard for the clock as she speaks.*)

ETHEL. Well, you've taken your time, I must say. (*She crosses to the mantel with the clock.*) We thought something 'ad 'appened to you. (*She puts the clock on the mantel and returns to the crate* R.C.)

SYLVIA (*below the crate* C.). I'd like to see you any quicker with a lot like that to carry. (*She groans.*) Oo, my poor back. (*She sits on the* L. *end of the crate* C.)

MRS. FLINT. It was your feet this afternoon.

SYLVIA (*snappily*). Well, it's me back now, so there.

ETHEL (*gathering up the parcel*). I'll take this into the kitchen.

SYLVIA. This house smells a bit damp, if you ask me.

ETHEL (*as she goes out*). All houses smell damp when you first move into 'em.

SYLVIA. Oh dear, I thought I was going to have one of my attacks just as I turned into Abbeville Road. I 'ad to lean against a pillar-box.

MRS. FLINT. I suppose you didn't think to remember my peppermints ?

SYLVIA. Yes, I did. They're in my bag. (*She fumbles in her bag.*) Here . . . (*She rises and goes to* MRS. FLINT.)

(*Hammering is heard upstairs.*)

MRS. FLINT (*taking them*). Well, thank 'eaven for small mercies—— Want one ?

SYLVIA. No, thanks, I daren't. (*Crossing to* L. *of the crate* R.C.) What's that hammering ?

MRS. FLINT. Frank. 'E's putting up the curtains in the front bedroom.

SYLVIA (*sitting in front of the crate* R.C.). I shall be glad when we're settled in, and no mistake. What a day !

ETHEL (*re-entering* R.). There's no opener !

MRS. FLINT. Frank's got one on his penknife.

ETHEL (*going into the hall and shouting*). Frank—Frank !

FRANK (*upstairs*). What's up ?

ETHEL. Chuck us down your penknife, we want the opener for the baked beans.

FRANK. 'Arf a mo' . . . here you are . . . coming down.

(*There is a moment's pause, and then the penknife falls at* ETHEL'S *feet. She comes back into the room to the crate* R.C.)

ETHEL. Here, Syl, go and fix 'em, there's a dear. I've got to get this room straight. Mother, you might go and help her. I've laid half the table and the saucepans are on the floor by the dresser.

SYLVIA (*taking the opener*). No peace for the wicked.

(*She exits* R.)

ETHEL (*picking up paper and putting it back in the crate*). Go on, Mother, you've sat there quite long enough.

(MRS. FLINT *rises.*)

MRS. FLINT (*crossing above the crate*). We ought to have kept Gladys an extra day and made her 'elp us with the move . . .

ETHEL. Gladys was more trouble than she was worth. I'd rather do for myself. (*She goes* R. *with the waste basket.*)

MRS. FLINT (*turning at the door*). All very fine for you. You're a young woman—wait till you get to my age . . .

(*She goes out.*)

ETHEL. Go on, Mother—I'll be in in a minute. (*Coming down to the door.*) I put the butter on the window-sill.

(ETHEL, *left alone, continues straightening the room, putting a cushion on the chair* L. *and moving the coal scuttle to the hearth. She hums a little song to herself as she does so. After a few moments* FRANK *comes in. He is an ordinary-looking man of thirty-five. He carries a hammer and a bag of tintacks. These he puts down on the sideboard.*)

FRANK. I just tacked 'em up for the time being. We'll 'ave to take 'em down again when the blinds come.

ETHEL (*crossing up to the windows*). Supper'll be ready soon. (*Untying the curtains* L. *of the window.*)

FRANK. You look tired. You've been doing too much.

ETHEL. Don't talk so silly.

FRANK (*crossing up* R. *of* ETHEL). You've been at it all day, you know.

ETHEL. What do you expect me to do—sit down by the fire and read a nice book ?

FRANK (*humorously*). All right, snappy ! (*He moves out just beyond the windows, looking off* R.) They haven't 'arf left that garden in a mess. Wait till I get after it. Here, look.

(ETHEL *joins him.*)

Bit of luck about that may-tree, isn't it ?

ETHEL. I never noticed it.

FRANK. You wouldn't.

ETHEL (*leaving him and coming in, to* R. *of the windows*). Fat lot of time I've had to stand around looking at may-trees. (*She unties the* R. *curtain.*)

FRANK (*turning back into the room*). Where's Percy ? (*He moves to the fire* L.)

ETHEL (*coming down to above the crate* C.). He started miaouing his 'ead off the moment we got here, so I let him out. He's up to no good, I shouldn't wonder.

FRANK. We ought to have 'ad him arranged when he was little.

ETHEL. Oh, Frank . . . (*She looks around the room.*) D'you like it ?

FRANK (*with his back to her, looking for matches*). Like what ?

(ETHEL *sits on the chest* C., *with her back to the audience.*)

ETHEL. The house, silly, you haven't said a word.

FRANK (*turning*). Of course I like it. (*Lighting a cigarette.*)

ETHEL. I can't hardly believe it, you know, not really, it's all been so quick. You being demobbed and coming home and getting the job through Mr. Baxter and now here we are moved in all inside of six weeks !

FRANK. Good old Baxter. We ought to drink his health.

ETHEL. We 'aven't got anything to drink it in except Sylvia's Wincarnis.

FRANK (*strolling to* L. *of the crate* C.). Well, 'e'll 'ave to take the will for the deed.

ETHEL. Oh, dear !

FRANK. What's up ? (*He sits on the crate facing down stage.*)

ETHEL. I don't know—— (*Turning to look at* FRANK.) I just can't get over not having that awful weight on me mind all the time.

FRANK. How d'you mean ?

ETHEL. Oh, you know.

FRANK (*turning towards her*). Me perishing on a field of slaughter ? What a chance !

ETHEL. There was a chance every minute of every day for four years and don't you forget it. I used to feel sick every time the postman came, every time the bell rang.

FRANK. Well, there's no sense in going on about it now, it's all over and done with.

ETHEL. We're lucky. It isn't so over and done with for some people. (*Rising, she goes to* L. *of the crate* R.C.) Look at poor old Mrs. Worsley, two sons gone and her husband, nothing left to live for, and Mrs. Cross with that boy she was so proud of done in for life, can't even feed himself properly. We're lucky all right, we ought to be grateful . . .

FRANK. Who to ?

ETHEL (*coming down to above the crate* C.). Now then, Frank . . .

FRANK. All right, I won't start any arguments—you can say your prayers till kingdom come if you like, but you can't expect me to, not after all I've seen. I don't 'old with a God who just singles a few out to be nice to, and lets all the others rot. 'E can get on with it for all I care.

ETHEL (*sitting above the crate* C.). It's wrong to talk like that, Frank ; it's blasphemy.

FRANK. Sorry, old girl. I've got to talk the way I feel.

ETHEL. Well, I think you ought to feel different from what you do.

FRANK. That's as may be, but you can't 'elp your feelings, can you ? I'm back, aren't I ? That's a fact. Instead of lying out there dead in a shell-'ole I'm sitting 'ere alive in Number Seventeen, Sycamore Road, Clapham Common. That's another fact. It's nobody's fault, not mine or yours or God's or anyone's, it just 'appened like that.

ETHEL. You went to the war because it was your duty and it's no use you pretending you didn't.

FRANK (*rising and crossing* L. *to the fire*). I went to the war because I wanted to.

ETHEL. Would you go again ?

FRANK (*turning*). I expect so.

ETHEL (*almost crying*). I wouldn't let you, see ? Not again ! I'd rather kill you with my own hands.

FRANK. That'd be just plain silly.

ETHEL (*rising and breaking up* C.). You give me a headache talking like that, it doesn't make sense. (*She turns to face him.*)

FRANK. What does make sense, I'd like to know ?

ETHEL (*heatedly*). Lots of things. (*Crossing down to him* L.) There's me and the children, isn't there ? There's your job, there's this house and the life we've got to live in it, and you spoil everything by talking about war and saying you'd go again if anyone asked you to . . .

FRANK. I never said that at all.

ETHEL (*moving to* C.). Oh yes, you did, you know you did, and I just can't bear to think of it (*facing him*)—not after all I've been through, waiting for you and wondering about you— it's cruel to make me even think of it.

FRANK. What's the use of upsetting yourself ? There isn't going to be another war, anyway.

ETHEL. There'll always be wars as long as men are such fools as to want to go to them.

FRANK (*moving slowly towards her*). Well, let's stop talking about it now, shall we ? Everything's all right. You're here, I'm here, the children are fine, except for Queenie's tonsils, and we've got a home of our own at last. Everything's more than all right, it's wonderful.

ETHEL (*sinking on the chest* C., *facing up stage*). Oh, Frank . . .

FRANK (*sitting on her* L., *facing down*). Poor old girl—living four years with your mother can't 'ave been all jam, I will say. I think I was better off in the trenches.

ETHEL (*muffled*). You ought to be ashamed, saying such things.

FRANK. Oh, your mother's all right in her way, but that house in Battersea—oh dear ! It gave me the willies after five weeks, let alone four years. At least we've got a bath now that doesn't scratch the hide off of you.

ETHEL. Lend me your 'anky.

FRANK (*giving her his handkerchief*). Here you are.

ETHEL (*blowing her nose*). I must go and 'elp Mother, and Syl with the supper.

FRANK (*turning her round*). 'Ere, let's have a look at you.

ETHEL. What for ?

FRANK. Just to see what's 'appened to your face. I don't seem to 'ave 'ad time for a really good look since I've been back.

ETHEL. Stop it . . . leave off . . .

FRANK. 'Old still a minute.

ETHEL. Now see here, Frank Gibbons . . . (*She wriggles, but without conviction.*)

FRANK. Well, it's not a bad face as faces go, I will say . . .

ETHEL. Thanks very much, I'm sure.

FRANK. And of course it's not quite as young as it was when I married it . . .

ETHEL. Leave 'old of me !

FRANK. But still, taken by and large, I wouldn't change it ! I might wipe some of the dirt off the side of it, but I wouldn't change it !

ETHEL (*struggling to get up*). Dirt—where ?

FRANK. I thought that would rouse you. (*Firmly.*) Keep still—'ere—— (*He rubs the side of her face with his handkerchief.*) That's better—now then——

ETHEL. Now then what ?

FRANK. Give us a kiss.

ETHEL. I'll do no such thing.

FRANK. Why not, may I ask ?

ETHEL. Because we haven't got no time for fooling about and well you know it . . .

FRANK. Oh—turning nasty, are we ? We'll soon see about that.

ETHEL. Frank Gibbons !——

FRANK (*kissing her firmly*). Shut up.

(*At this moment,* BOB MITCHELL, *a pleasant-looking man of thirty-seven, appears at the french windows* C., *and taps politely.* FRANK *breaks away, slightly to* L., *and* ETHEL *a pace down* R.)

Just in time, or born in the vestry.

BOB. I hope I don't intrude ?

ETHEL. Oh, dear !

BOB (*moving down* C.). I live at number fifteen next door, and my missus and I thought if you needed anything in the way of groceries or what-not . . .

FRANK (*staring at him*). Well, I'll be damned !

ETHEL. Frank !

FRANK. Mitchell—Bob Mitchell !

BOB (*a little puzzled*). That's right.

FRANK. Don't you remember me—Frank Gibbons, the Buffs, B Company, Festubert, nineteen-fifteen ?

BOB. My God ! It's old Gibbo !

(*They rush at each other, shake hands and slap each other on the back* L.C.)

ETHEL. Well, I never . . .

FRANK. You old son of a gun . . .

BOB. My God, I thought you was dead as mutton after that night attack . . . when we'd gone on to Givenchy and left your lot in the mud . . .

FRANK. Me dead as mutton! I'm tougher than that—only one small 'ole through me leg in four years . . . How did you make out?

BOB. Not so bad—got gassed in nineteen-seventeen, but I'm all right now—made me chest a bit weak, that's all.

FRANK. Well, I'll say it's a small world and no mistake.

ETHEL. Don't you think you'd better introduce me, Frank?

FRANK. Of course—— This is my wife, Ethel . . . Bob Mitchell.

BOB. Pleased to meet you, Mrs. Gibbons.

ETHEL. It's a pleasure, I'm sure.

(They shake hands.)

BOB. What a coincidence—I can't get over it.

FRANK. How long have you been here?

BOB. Over a year now—we took the house when I got me discharge in March nineteen-eighteen. I couldn't do any work for a while, but I had me pension and Nora, that's my missus, had a little put by, but now I'm doing fine—in the insurance business. *(He pauses, then to* ETHEL.) Nora would have come herself, but she's a bit under the weather to-night. You see, we're expecting a little stranger almost any day now, and . . .

ETHEL. It's not her first, I hope.

BOB. Oh no—we've got a boy of fourteen, he wants to be a sailor, and we had a girl too, but she died in nineteen-sixteen just after I'd gone back after me first leave . . .

FRANK. What a coincidence! What a coincidence! After four bloody years.

ETHEL. Frank!

FRANK. Well, if they weren't bloody, nothing was!

ETHEL. I'm afraid we haven't anything to offer you, Mr. Mitchell—you see, everything's upside down . . .

FRANK. He can stay and have whatever we're 'aving.

BOB. No, thanks all the same—I'll have to be getting back to Nora.

FRANK. We've got to celebrate this somehow . . .

BOB *(moving up)*. I've got a bottle of Johnnie Walker next door—it won't take a minute . . .

ETHEL. You two stay here—I'll go and fetch Sylvia's Wincarnis.

(She runs out R.)

FRANK. Oh, dear!

BOB. It won't take me a minute to get the whisky . . .

FRANK. Here, whose dugout d'you think this is ?   I'll pop in and 'ave one with you later.   Have a cigarette ?

BOB. Ta.   Have you got a job yet ?

(*They move to the crate* c.)

FRANK. Yes—I had a bit of luck—a chap called Baxter in my regiment, he was drafted out to Arras in February nineteen-seventeen and before the war he was running a sort of travel agency in Oxford Street—well, he got a Blighty one and was invalided 'ome, and believe it or not, 'e was the first one I run into when I got back last April.   He'd started his business again, and things were beginning to pick up, so he gave me a job. (*He sits on the crate down* L.)

BOB. Travel Agency—whew !

FRANK. Tours of the battlefields, I'll thank you !

BOB (*laughing*). That's a good one. (*He sits on the crate* c., *facing* FRANK.)

FRANK. Some people certainly do have queer ways of enjoying themselves.

BOB. You've got kids, haven't you ?   I remember you talking about them.

FRANK. Yes, three.   Two girls and a boy.   They're with Ethel's aunt in Broadstairs.   We didn't want them under our feet while we were moving in.

BOB. How old are they ?

FRANK. Reg, that's the boy, 'e's twelve ; Queenie's thirteen, and Vi's fourteen.

BOB. My Billy's getting on for fifteen.

FRANK. Seems funny, this, doesn't it ?   When you think of the last time we 'ad a jaw—remember that canteen ?

BOB. Just before Christmas, wasn't it ?   The night before you went up to the line.   What was her name, that Lady Something-or-other behind the bar, the one that called you her poor dear . . .

FRANK. What was it ?—I can see her now—a fair knock-out, she was.

BOB. What happened to old Shorty ?

FRANK. You mean the little fat chap with red hair in my company ?

BOB. That's him.

FRANK. 'E got 'is on the Somme, poor bastard, 'adn't been out of the trench two seconds when, wallop, out 'e went !

BOB. Nice and quick and no hurt feelings.

FRANK. You've said it.

(ETHEL *re-enters* R., *with a bottle of Wincarni˄ and two glasses.*
BOB *and* FRANK *rise.*)

ETHEL. Here you are—supper will be ready in a minute.

(*She puts the bottle and glasses on the crate* c.)   Are you sure you won't stay and take pot luck with us, Mr. Mitchell ?

BOB.   Thanks very much, Mrs. Gibbons, but I really must get back.

ETHEL.   Will you ask your wife when it would be convenient for me to pop in and see her ?

BOB.   Any time—any time at all.

ETHEL.   Well, I'll be saying good night, Mr. Mitchell.

FRANK.   Aren't you going to have a drop ?

ETHEL.   No, dear, it would spoil my supper—don't be long.

BOB.   Don't forget—if there's anything you're wanting——

ETHEL.   Thank you very much, I'm sure.   Good night.

BOB.   Good night.

(ETHEL *goes out.*   FRANK *pours out the Wincarnis.*)

FRANK (*handing a glass to* BOB).   Here you are, old man.

BOB.   Thanks.

FRANK.   It tastes a bit funny, but it's better than nothing.

BOB.   Happy days !

FRANK.   Happy days !

They drink as—

The lights fade and the CURTAIN *falls.*

SCENE 2

TIME.—*December,* 1925.

It is about three o'clock on Christmas afternoon.   Christmas dinner is over.

There is a dining-table R.C.   (*See the Ground Plan.*)   *Nine chairs are set at the table—one at each end, four above, and three below.   There is an armchair* L.C., *above the fire (this may be of a more modern type than in Scene* 1).   *The tub chair is* L., *below the fire.   The settee is up* L., *against the back wall, while the " whatnot " is up stage on the* R. *of the windows.   The sideboard* R., *as before.   A pedestal, with* MRS. FLINT'S *work-basket, is slightly above and to the* L. *of the armchair above the fire.   The revolving book-stand is down* L.   *Another small table and a chair, down* R., *are below the door.*

At the table are seated :

REG, *at the* L. *end.*

SAM LEADBITTER, *at the* R. *end.*

QUEENIE, *above the table, second chair from the* R.

PHYLLIS BLAKE, *above, extreme* L. *chair.*

VI *is below the table, extreme* R. *chair.*

All are wearing paper hats.

The chairs of FRANK, ETHEL, SYLVIA *and* MRS. FLINT *are*

*empty as they have retired to the rarely used drawing-room in order
to leave the young people alone.*

Vi *is a pleasant, nondescript girl of twenty ;* Queenie, *who
is a year younger, is prettier and a trifle flashy.* Reg, *aged
eighteen, is a nice-looking, intelligent boy.* Sam Leadbitter,
who is about a year older than Reg, *is rather farouche in appearance. He is intense, without much humour, and slightly aware
of intellectual superiority.* Reg *admires him extravagantly.*
Phyllis Blake, *who is a friend of* Queenie's, *is a gentle,
matter-of-fact girl of eighteen.*

As the Curtain *rises,* Reg *is starting to make a speech.*
(Note.—*The french windows and the door are closed, and the
curtains are half-drawn.*)

Reg. . . . I will now propose a toast to the two strangers
within our gates . . .

Queenie. 'Ark at him !

Vi. Shut up, Queenie.

Reg (*ignoring the interruption*). Welcome, thrice welcome,
Sam Leadbitter and Phyllis Blake. (*He raises his glass of port
and makes a signal for everyone to drink.*)

Queenie. You ought to have mentioned the lady first.

Reg (*grandly*). Sweeping aside the annoying interruptions of
my young sister, who is being far too bossy as usual, I will now
call upon my old and valued friend, Sam Leadbitter, to say a
few words . . .

Queenie. Old and valued friend ! You've only known 'im
since August Bank Holiday—chuck us the nut-crackers, Phyl——

Vi. Speech—speech—speech ! Oh, dear ! (*She giggles.*)

Reg. Come on, Sam.

Queenie. Get it off your chest, Sam, Edie'll be in to clear
in a minute.

(*Amid loud applause* Sam *rises to his feet.*)

Sam. Ladies and gentlemen—Comrades——

Queenie. Make up your mind.

Reg. You're asking for it, you know, Queenie, and if you
don't shut up being saucy, you'll get it ! Go on, Sam, don't take
no notice of her.

Sam. Comrades—— In thanking you for your kind hos-
pitality on this festive day, I would like to say that it is both
a pleasure and a privilege to be here . . .

Queenie. Hear—hear——

Sam. Though as you know, holding the views I do, it's really
against my principles to hobnob to any great extent with the
bourgeoisie . . .

Queenie. What's that ?

Vi. I think it means common in a nice way.

REG. Order!

SAM. I cannot but feel that to-day, what with being Christmas and one thing and another, it would be but right and proper to put aside all prejudice and class hatred . . .

QUEENIE. Very nice of you, I'm sure.

SAM. . . . As you well know, there are millions and millions of homes in this country to-day where Christmas is naught but a mockery, where there is neither warmth nor food nor even the bare necessities of life, where little children, old before their time, huddle round a fireless grate . . .

QUEENIE. They'd be just as well off if they stayed in the middle of the room then, wouldn't they?

REG. *Shut up*, Queenie, Sam's quite right.

SAM (*sternly*). That sort of remark, Queenie, springs from complacency, arrogance and a full stomach!

QUEENIE. You leave my stomach out of it!

SAM (*warming up*). It is people like you, apathetic, unthinking, docile supporters of a capitalistic system which is a disgrace to civilization, who are responsible for at least three-quarters of the cruel suffering of the world! It doesn't matter to you that the greatest struggle for the betterment of mankind that has ever been in the history of the world is going on under your noses! Oh dear no, you haven't even noticed it, you're too busy getting all weepy about Rudolph Valentino to spare any tears for the workers of the world whose whole lives are made hideous by oppression, injustice and capitalistic greed!

VI. Don't get excited, Sam, Queenie didn't mean it.

SAM (*violently*). I am not excited. Queenie doesn't mean anything to me, anyway . . .

QUEENIE. Pardon me, all, while I go and commit suicide!

SAM. . . . But what she represents, what she symbolizes, means a great deal. She is only one of the millions who, when the great day comes, will be swept out of existence like so much chaff on the wind . . .

QUEENIE. Well, it's nice to know, isn't it?

SAM (*sitting down abruptly*). I've said my say, thank you very much.

REG (*dutifully*). Hear, hear . . . bravo!

QUEENIE. I don't know what you're saying bravo about, I'm sure. I think Sam's been very rude.

REG. You don't understand, Queenie; if you did, you wouldn't have kept interrupting all the time and trying to be funny. Sam's quite right in everything he says, only you just haven't got enough sense to see it.

QUEENIE. I suppose you understand all of it, don't you?

REG. No, I don't, but I'm trying to.

QUEENIE. I suppose we shall soon be having *you* standing up on a soap-box in Hyde Park and making a fathead of yourself!

Vi. Run and tell Edie we're ready for her to clear now, Queenie, say we'll help her.

(QUEENIE *rises*.)

The boys can go into the front-room, we've left Mum and Dad and Granny alone quite long enough.

REG (*with sarcasm*). Maybe if we asked her nicely, Aunt Sylvia'd sing us the Indian Love Lyrics !

Vi. And don't talk in that tone about poor Aunt Sylvia, she's not feeling well.

QUEENIE (*going out of the room*). She never is.

REG (*rising*). Come on, Sam. Come up to my room for a minute and have a cigarette.

Vi. Better not let your father catch you.

SAM (*rising*). I'm sorry if I was rude, Vi.

VI (*beginning to pile up the plates*). It doesn't matter, Sam, only you can't expect everybody in the world to feel just the same as you do, you know.

REG (*hotly*). Sam's got more knowledge and intelligence than all of us put together.

Vi. If that's the case, it wouldn't do him any harm to remember it once in a while and not shout so much.

REG (*irritably*). Come on, Sam.

(*He slams out of the room, followed, rather sheepishly, by* SAM.)

PHYLLIS. Can I help, Vi ?

Vi. Yes, Phyl, you might put the preserved fruits in the sideboard cupboard, the sweets can go in there too, but leave one dish out to take into the front room.

PHYLLIS (*complying*). Sam got quite upset, didn't he ?

Vi. He's a bit Bolshie, that's all that's the matter with him.

PHYLLIS. I didn't understand half of what he was talking about.

Vi. I don't expect he understood much of it himself.

PHYLLIS. Reg thinks he's wonderful.

Vi. Reg thinks anybody who can use a few long words is wonderful. He'll soon get over it.

(QUEENIE *re-enters, followed by* EDIE, *with a tray.* EDIE *is rather an unkempt girl of about twenty-five. During the following scene she and the girls manage to clear the table, change the table-cloths and generally tidy up the room.*)

QUEENIE. Has Trotsky gone upstairs ?

VI (*putting two chairs up either side of the whatnot*). You were awful, Queenie ; if you hadn't of gone on at him the way you did, he wouldn't have got so excited.

QUEENIE (*busying herself*). Silly great fool.

Vi. You needn't stay and wash up, Edie, you can slip along home. We can do it later. (*She comes down* L. *of* Edie.)

Edie. Thanks very much.

Vi. How's your father's neck ?

Edie. Mother was up all night poulticing it, but it was still paining him terrible when I left this morning.

Phyllis. They say if you have one you generally have seven.

Edie. Well, this is 'is third, so we only got four more to go.

Vi (*piling things on to the tray*). There's some crackers left in the box in the sideboard—you might care to take them home to your little brother.

Edie (*finding them*). Thanks ever so.

Queenie. Here—you can balance them on the top—that's right.

(*She balances the box of crackers on the top of the loaded tray and Edie staggers out of the room with it. Queenie goes to the sideboard as Vi and Phyllis fold up the tablecloth between them. Queenie brings down the day cloth from the sideboard to the table and Vi takes the white cloth up to the sideboard and puts it away.*)

Phyllis (*above the* L. *end of the table*). It has been nice you letting me spend my Christmas Day with you. I don't know what I'd have done all by myself in that house in Wandsworth with Auntie ill and everything.

(*She helps Queenie, who is now at the* R. *end, to put on the day cloth.*)

Vi (*crossing to* L.). Is she any better ?

Phyllis. No, she just goes on about the same. Mrs. Watts is looking after her until seven, so I don't have to get back till about then.

Queenie (R. *of the table, helping* Phyllis *to put on the day tablecloth*). One of our girls at the shop's mother has been bedridden for five years—can't even get up to wash herself. Just think of that !

Phyllis. What some people go through !

(*There is the sound of a tap at the window.*)

Queenie (*looking towards the window*). Good heavens, what's that ?

(*Vi goes to the window and opens it for Billy. It is still more or less daylight, but there is a fog, so the outlook is rather gloomy. Billy Mitchell steps into the room. He is a nice-looking boy of about twenty-one. He is in sailor's rig only without his cap.*)

Vi. Billy, what a surprise ! I thought you was going back this morning.

BILLY (*coming down* L.C.). No, not till to-night. Hallo—Queen——

QUEENIE (*above the centre of the table*). Hallo.

(VI *is closing the window.*)

BILLY. Better leave the window on the latch, Dad'll be in in a minute.

VI (*coming down* L. *of* BILLY, *introducing*). Do you know Miss Blake . . . Mr. Mitchell.

BILLY (*shaking hands*). Pleased to meet you.

QUEENIE. Have a choc?

(PHYLLIS *sits on the chair* L. *of the table.* VI *crosses down to the chair below the fire.*)

BILLY. No, thanks. I've been eating my head off. Where's Reg?

VI. Upstairs with Sam. (*She sits, down* L.)

BILLY. Oh, he's here, is he?

QUEENIE. I'll say he is. I wonder you didn't hear him. He's been bellowing like a bull. (*She sits on a chair above the table.*)

BILLY (*sitting in the chair above the fire*). Down with the dirty capitalists?

QUEENIE. That's right.

BILLY. I know all that stuff by heart—we got a couple of 'em in my ship, not bad chaps really, you know, just got everything a bit cock-eyed, that's all.

PHYLLIS. It must be lovely being a sailor.

BILLY. Well, I wouldn't go so far as to say lovely, exactly, but it's not bad, and you do get about. Join the Navy and see the world, you know.

QUEENIE. Go on—you've never been further than Southsea!

BILLY (*cheerfully*). Lots of time. Next year I'll probably be sent to the China station—think of that!

QUEENIE. Well, drop us a p.c. saying you've arrived safely.

PHYLLIS. China station sounds funny, doesn't it? Like as though it was on the Underground! (*She giggles.*)

VI. We ought to go into the front-room now, Mum'll be wondering what's happened to us.

BILLY. Be a sport and go on in then, Vi, I want to talk to Queenie a minute.

VI. Oh, so that's how it is, is it?

QUEENIE. I don't know what you're talking about, I'm sure.

(VI *rises, and crosses* R., *below the table.*)

VI (*as she crosses*). Come on, Phyl, we know when we're not wanted.

(PHYLLIS *rises, goes to the door* R., VI *following.*)

QUEENIE (*rising*). I don't see why we don't all go.

BILLY. I want to talk to you a minute, I just said so, didn't I ?

(PHYLLIS *exits.* VI *checks,* R. *of the table, to select a chocolate.*)

QUEENIE. Maybe I don't want to talk to you !

BILLY. Well, if you're going to be high and mighty about it, it's all right with me. (*He rises, to the fire.*) I only thought that as I was going back to duty to-night that . . .

VI (*moving to the door*). Of course Queenie'll stay for a minute, Billy, she's only putting on airs.

QUEENIE. You mind your own business, Vi Gibbons. I'll talk to who I like when I like.

VI. Well, nobody's stopping you . . . See you later, Billy ; don't go without saying good-bye to Mum and Dad.

BILLY. You bet I won't.

(VI *exits* R., *closing the door.* QUEENIE *replaces the chairs about the table, and puts the palm on the centre of it.*)

QUEENIE (L. *of the centre of the table*). Well ?

BILLY (*grinning*). Well, what ?

QUEENIE (*moving to* L.C.). What is it you're so keen to talk to me about ?

BILLY. I don't rightly know now, you being so upsiedupsie's put it right out of my head.

QUEENIE. I beg your pardon, I'm sure. (*She sits on the armchair above the fire* L.)

BILLY. Don't mention it—all in the day's work.

QUEENIE. Fancy asking Vi and Phyl to go out and leave us alone, you ought to have known better. I shall never hear the last of it.

BILLY. Oh, so that's what's worrying you, is it ?

QUEENIE (*shrugging her shoulders*). It's not worrying me at all, I just thought it sounded sort of silly, that's all.

BILLY (*crossing to* L. *of the table*). I don't see what's silly about it. (*Turning to face her.*) Vi knows we went to the Majestic on Friday night, and she saw us with her own eyes walking down Elm Park Road on Sunday—she must guess there's something doing.

QUEENIE. Well, if she does she's wrong, so there. There isn't.

BILLY. 'Ere, 'arf a minute—what's got into you, anyway ? I haven't done anything wrong, have I ?

QUEENIE. I don't like being taken for granted ; no girl does.

BILLY (*moving to* R. *of the armchair*). How d'you mean, taken for granted ? You can't hold hands with someone all through " Desert Love " and the next minute expect them to treat you like the Empress of Russia !

QUEENIE. Oh, don't talk so silly.

BILLY. It's you that's silly.

QUEENIE (*rising and crossing below him to the table* R.C.). I think we'd better go into the front-room.

BILLY (*turning away ; breaking* L.). All right, if that's the way you feel.

QUEENIE (*above the* L. *end of the table*). Well, we're not doing much good here, are we ? Just nagging at each other.

BILLY. Who started it ?

QUEENIE. Oh—come on.

BILLY (*downcast*). Aren't you going to kiss me good-bye ? We shan't be able to in there.

QUEENIE. I should think not, indeed.

BILLY (*crossing to* L. *of* QUEENIE). Look here, Queenie, if you think I oughtn't to have said that about wanting to talk to you alone in front of Vi, I'm sorry, see ? I can't say more than that, now can I ?

QUEENIE (*looking down*). No, I suppose not.

BILLY. Well then !

QUEENIE (*with an imperceptible movement towards him*). Oh, all right . . .

(BILLY *takes her in his arms and kisses her.*)

BILLY (*gently*). I do love you, Queenie—you know that, don't you ?

QUEENIE (*resting her head on his shoulder*). Yes.

BILLY. And I wouldn't do anything to upset you—that is, not meaning to—you know that too, don't you ?

QUEENIE. Oh, Billy—I wish you weren't going back so soon.

BILLY. Will you write to me every now and again ? Even if it's only a post-card ?

QUEENIE. If you'll write to me.

BILLY. That's easy. Promise ?

QUEENIE. Yes—cross my heart.

BILLY (*taking her hands*). You're the sweetest girl I ever met in all my life or ever will meet, either.

QUEENIE. That's easy to say, but how do you know ?

(BILLY *puts his arm round her and leads her to the fire.*)

BILLY. Never you mind, it's true. I've been thinking about you all the time, ever since that sick leave I had at Whitsun, when we went to Richmond Park—do you remember ?

QUEENIE. Of course I do.

BILLY. A little later on, when I'm earning a bit more, do you think we might have a shot at getting married ?

QUEENIE (*turning away*). Oh, Bill, how do I know—you might be in China or anywhere—you might have forgotten all about me by then. (*To the chair* L. *of the table.*)

BILLY. More likely to be the other way round. A pretty kid like you, working at being a manicurist, talking to all sorts of different fellows all day long . . .

QUEENIE. It isn't all jam being a sailor's wife, is it ?

BILLY. It wouldn't be so bad, if I get me promotion all right and get on—(*moving towards her*) don't say anything now, just think it over . . .

QUEENIE (*with a rush*). Oh, Billy, I wouldn't be the right sort of wife for you, really I wouldn't. (*Moving below the table to the* R. *end.*) I want too much—I'm always thinking about the kind of things I want and they wouldn't be the kind of things you'd want me to want.

BILLY. How do you mean ?

QUEENIE. Oh, I know it sounds silly, but I'm not like Vi ; she's a quiet one ; I'm different. (*She sits on the table at the* R. *end.*) Mum sometimes says that all I think of is having a good time, but it isn't only that . . .

BILLY (*coming down* C., *above the* L. *end of the table*). I don't see no harm in wanting to have a good time—that's what everybody wants in one way or another.

QUEENIE. I'll tell you something awful. I hate living here, I hate living in a house that's exactly like hundreds of other houses. I hate coming home from work in the Tube. I hate washing up and helping Mum darn Dad's socks and listening to Aunt Sylvia keeping on about how ill she is all the time, and what's more I know why I hate it too, it's because it's all so common ! There ! (*Getting off the table.*) I expect you'll think I'm getting above myself, and I wouldn't blame you—maybe I am, but I can't help it (*crossing above the table to him at* C.) that's why I don't think I'd be a good wife for you, however much I loved you—and I do . . . I really do . . . Oh, Billy . . . (*She bursts into tears.*)

BILLY (*putting his arms round her*). Here, hold on, dear, there isn't anything to cry about—*I* know what you mean all right, it's only natural that you should feel that way about things.

QUEENIE. You don't think I'm awful then, do you ? And mean ?

BILLY. Of course I don't—come on now, cheer up ; you don't want to have red eyes on Christmas Day, do you ?

QUEENIE (*dabbing her eyes with her handkerchief*). I'm sorry, Bill, please forgive me . . .

(*She suddenly kisses him and runs out of the room.* BILLY *stands looking after her in perplexity for a moment, and then with a sigh turns away* L. *and goes up towards the window. He has nearly reached it when* FRANK *comes in* R. *He hasn't really changed very much in the last six years. His figure is perhaps a shade thicker and his hair a shade greyer and thinner. At the*

moment he is still wearing the paper hat he got out of a cracker.
BILLY *turns to face down* R.)

FRANK.   Billy !   What are you doing in here all by yourself ?

BILLY.   I've been talking to Queenie.

FRANK (*moving in below the table*).   Was that her rushing upstairs just now ?

BILLY.   Yes—I think it was.

FRANK (*quizzically*).   Oh, I see.   (*He crosses to the fire.*)

BILLY (*coming down a little*).   I just popped in to say good-bye——

FRANK (*turning at the fireplace*).   A bit miserable having to go back to work on Christmas night, isn't it ?

BILLY (*above the* L. *end of the table*).   Oh, I dunno—it's all right once you're there.

FRANK.   How old are you now, Billy ?

BILLY.   Getting on for twenty-one.

FRANK.   Wish I was.

BILLY (*coming to* L.C.—*with an effort*).   Mr. Gibbons——

FRANK.   Yes, son ?

BILLY.   If in two or three years' time when I've worked my way up a bit Queenie and me get married, would you mind ?

FRANK.   If Queenie wanted to, it wouldn't matter whether I minded or not.   She'd get her own way, she always does.

BILLY (*ruefully*).   She's certainly got a will of her own all right.

FRANK.   Anyway, a lot can happen between now and three years.

BILLY (*sitting on the* R. *arm of the armchair*).   You see I leave the ship I'm in now round about April and next commission I'll probably be drafted for foreign service.   By the time I get back, I ought to be drawing higher pay if I've been behaving myself.

FRANK.   What does Queenie think about it ?

BILLY.   That's the trouble—I think she thinks that being a sailor's wife might be rather hard going . . .

FRANK.   She likes having a good time, our Queenie, but maybe she'll calm down later on, here's hoping, anyhow.

BILLY.   If you get a chance, Mr. Gibbons, you might put in a good word for me every now and again.

FRANK (*smiling*).   Righto, son, I'll do my best.

BILLY.   Thanks, Mr. Gibbons.   (*Rising.*)   I think I'll be getting along now.   Mother always gets a bit depressed on my last day of leave.

FRANK.   How is she ?

BILLY.   As well as can be expected.

FRANK.   Aren't you going into the front-room ?

BILLY.   I'd rather not, if you don't mind.

FRANK. All right—I'll say good-bye for you.
BILLY. Thank you again, Mr. Gibbons.
FRANK. Go on, 'op it—good luck !

(*They shake hands solemnly.* BILLY *turns up* C., *and goes out through the french window.* FRANK, *left alone, takes a Gold Flake out of a packet in his pocket, lights it, and balances it on the edge of the mantelpiece while he puts some more coal on the fire. Then he settles himself comfortably in the armchair above the fire. From the drawing-room comes the sound of the piano and* SYLVIA's *voice singing " When I Am Dying." The door* R. *opens gently, and* ETHEL *slips into the room.*)

ETHEL. Frank, you are awful creeping out like that You knew Sylvia was going to sing.
FRANK. What about you ?
ETHEL (*crossing below the table*). I came to find you.
FRANK. Oh yes, we know all about that.
ETHEL (*at* L.C.). D'you want the light on ?
FRANK. No, it's all right like this—come and sit down.
ETHEL (*sitting in the chair below the fire* L.). Edie's gone home ; the girls are going to do the washing up after tea.
FRANK. Is Reg in there ?
ETHEL. Yes, he came in a minute ago with that Sam Leadbitter.
FRANK (*chuckling*). What's the betting they've been smoking themselves silly up in Reg's room ?
ETHEL. Well, it is Christmas. I don't think much of that Sam Leadbitter taken all round, he seems a bit soft to me.
FRANK. I wouldn't call him soft exactly.
ETHEL. Well, you know what I mean—all that talking big —he'll get himself into trouble one of these days, you mark my words.
FRANK. He'll grow out of it. I used to shoot me neck off to beat the band when I was his age.
ETHEL. Not like he does though, all that stuff about world revolution and the great day and down with everything—you had more sense than that. Anyhow, I wouldn't mind so much if it wasn't for Reg taking every word he says as gospel—we'll be having him with long hair and a red tie soon if we're not careful.
FRANK. I shouldn't say a word if I was you, let 'em get it out of their systems.
ETHEL. It is wrong, isn't it ? All that Bolshie business ?
FRANK. Oh, there's something to be said for it, there's always something to be said for everything. Where they go wrong is trying to get things done too quickly. We don't like doing things quickly in this country. It's like gardening, some-one once said we was a nation of gardeners, and they weren't far

wrong. We're used to planting things and watching them grow and looking out for changes in the weather . . .

ETHEL. You and your gardening !

FRANK. Well, it's true—think what a mess there'd be if all the flowers and vegetables and crops came popping up all in a minute—that's what all these social reformers are trying to do, trying to alter the way of things all at once. What works in other countries won't work in this one. We've got our own way of settling things ; it may be slow and it may be a bit dull, but it suits us all right and it always will.

(SYLVIA'S *voice is heard singing off.*)

ETHEL (*rising*). Oh, do listen to Sylvia, (*to up* L.C.) she's off on " Bird of Love Divine " now, and you know how it always makes Reg laugh !

FRANK. Poor old Sylvia !

ETHEL (*turning towards* FRANK). We ought to go back really, it'll be tea-time in a minute.

FRANK. It's cosy in here.

(ETHEL *sits on the* R. *arm of the armchair.*)

ETHEL (*settling herself against* FRANK). Getting quite dark, isn't it ?

They sit together in silence as—

The lights fade and the CURTAIN *falls.*

SCENE 3

TIME.—*May, 1926.*

It is late in the evening, about ten-thirty. The french windows are open as it is very warm. MRS. FLINT *is sitting in an armchair by the fireplace.* ETHEL, SYLVIA, VI *and* QUEENIE *are at the table having supper which consists of cold ham, tomatoes, cheese, pickles and tea.* ETHEL *is sitting* R. *of the table,* VI *above it, and* QUEENIE *below it.*)

ETHEL. . . . Run into the kitchen, Queenie, there's a dear, and see if the soup's all right. Dad ought to be home soon, it's getting on for eleven.

QUEENIE (*rising reluctantly*). All right, if my legs will get me that far.

ETHEL. When you've done that you'd better go to bed—you too, Vi, you must be dog tired, all that standing about . . .

QUEENIE (*as she goes*). I wonder if they'll open up the shop again to-morrow—I'll have to go along in the morning and see.

VI. Are you going to wait up for Dad, Mum ?

ETHEL. Yes, I'm all right—they said in Regent's Park his shift would be back before ten—I wish I hadn't missed him with those sandwiches. Seems silly trailing all that way for nothing . . .

SYLVIA. Feels sort of flat now, doesn't it ? It all being over, I mean.

MRS. FLINT. It's wicked, that's what it is, downright wicked, those strikers upsetting the whole country like that . . .

ETHEL. I wish Reg'd come home ; I wish I knew where he was.

VI. I'll give that Sam Leadbitter a piece of my mind when I see him. Encouraging Reg to make a fool of himself—I'll tell him off, you see if I don't.

ETHEL. Telling people off's no good, when they think they're in the right.

SYLVIA. I was talking to Mr. Rogers only a couple of weeks ago—his brother works up North, you know, and he said that conditions were something terrible, he did really.

MRS. FLINT. You and your Mr. Rogers.

SYLVIA (*facing* MRS. FLINT). He's been very kind to me and I like him, so there.

MRS. FLINT. Like him ! I should just think you did—we get nothing but Mr. Rogers this and Mr. Rogers that from morning till night. I'd like to know what Mrs. Rogers has to say about it, I must say.

SYLVIA. Now look here, Mrs. Flint, if you're insinuating . . .

MRS. FLINT. You give me a pain, Sylvia, really you do, the way you keep on about that man—just because he pays you a few shillings every now and again for designing them Christmas cards and calendars, you're doing nothing more nor less than throwing yourself at his head.

SYLVIA (*rising, furious*). Mrs. Flint, how can you !

ETHEL (*wearily*). Oh, do shut up, you two—I've got enough to think about without listening to you snapping at each other. Sylvia can go and live with Mr. Rogers for all I care.

SYLVIA (*behind her chair*). That's a nice way to talk, Ethel, I must say.

ETHEL. Now look here, Sylvia, I'm tired, see ? We're all tired. And what's more, I'm worried to death about Reg. I 'aven't slept properly for three nights wondering what's happened to him. If on top of all that I have to hear you and Mother go on nag, nag, nag at each other over nothing at all, I shall lose my temper, and that's a fact. You never stop, either of you, and I'm sick to death of it.

MRS. FLINT. I'm sure I haven't said anything.

ETHEL. Oh yes, you have. You're always giving Sylvia sly digs about Mr. Rogers. You know perfectly well Sylvia isn't strong enough to do any steady work, and the odd commissions she gets from that novelty shop come in very handy. If Mr. Rogers has taken a fancy to her, so much the better, she's old enough to look after herself, 'eaven knows, and if he murdered his wife and strangled his children and run off to Australia with her, it still wouldn't be anything to do with you, so shut up !

MRS. FLINT (*struggling to get out of her chair*). Help me up—help me up—I'm not going to stay here and be insulted by my own daughter.

ETHEL. You're not being insulted by anyone, be quiet.

SYLVIA. It's all my fault—I'm in the way in this house and I always have been and you needn't think I don't know it . . .

ETHEL. It's a pity you've stayed so long, then.

SYLVIA (*bursting into tears*). Oh, Ethel, how can you ! (*She sits in her chair.*) I'll leave to-morrow, I'll never set foot in the house again . . .

MRS. FLINT. And a good job too.

VI. Oh, don't cry, Auntie Sylvia, Mother didn't mean it. She's nervy to-night, we all are . . .

SYLVIA (*sobbing*). I don't care how nervy she is, if only I had my health and strength I'm sure I wouldn't have to be beholden to anybody.

MRS. FLINT. Health and strength indeed ! You're as strong as a cart-horse !

ETHEL. Take your grandmother up to bed, Vi, for God's sake.

VI (*rising and crossing to* L.). Come on, Granny—I'll help you upstairs . . .

ETHEL. Stop crying, Sylvia—I didn't mean what I said. I don't know which way to turn to-night what with one thing and another . . .

MRS. FLINT (*shaking* VI *off*). I can manage by myself, thank you.

(VI *turns a little up* L.C.)

SYLVIA. If you wished to hurt me, you've certainly succeeded——

ETHEL. Nobody wished to hurt you—do stop crying, you'll only give yourself one of your headaches . . .

(QUEENIE *comes into the room.*)

QUEENIE (*at the door*). What in the world's happening ? I thought the strikers had got in !

VI. It's only Auntie Sylvia and Granny, as usual.

(QUEENIE *moves above the table* R.C.)

SYLVIA. That's right, blame me ! Everything's always my fault.

MRS. FLINT. I'm an old woman and the sooner I'm dead the better—I know you're all itching to see me in my coffin . . .

VI (*moving towards her*). Don't talk so silly, Granny, come on upstairs.

MRS. FLINT. It's coming to something when your own flesh and blood turns on you as if you was a criminal . . .

VI. Never mind, Gran, it'll all be forgiven and forgotten in the morning . . .

(*She leads* MRS. FLINT *to down* R., *still talking. They exit* R. ETHEL *puts her head wearily down on her arms.* QUEENIE *goes to her.*)

QUEENIE. Have another cup of tea, Mum, it'll buck you up.

ETHEL. I'm all right.

QUEENIE. Here—I'll pour it out.

ETHEL. You'd better give your Aunt Sylvia a cup too.

SYLVIA (*bridling*). I don't want anyone to put themselves out on my account, I'm sure.

QUEENIE (*pouring out a cup of tea*). Nobody is, Aunt Sylvia. Here you are, the sugar's just by you. (*Pouring another cup.*) Here you are, Mum.

ETHEL. Thank you, dear. Now slip along up to bed, there's a good girl.

(SYLVIA *sips her tea.*)

QUEENIE. I'd rather wait till Dad comes, he can't be long now. (*She crosses* L.)

ETHEL. Very well.

SYLVIA (*with martyred politeness*). Would you like me to wait up for Frank, Ethel, and you go to bed ?

ETHEL. No, thanks, Sylvia—I couldn't sleep, anyway.

SYLVIA. I've been sleeping terribly badly lately, what with all the upset and the heat and everything . . .

ETHEL. Go on up now then and take an aspirin.

SYLVIA. I daren't, it always makes my heart go funny. Doctor Morgan says it does do that with some people. He gave me some tablets but I'm afraid they're not much good. I'll take two to-night just to see what happens.

ETHEL. I shouldn't overdo it if I was you.

SYLVIA. They're quite harmless. (*She rises.*) I'll take my tea up with me. (*She moves* R., *above the table.*)

ETHEL (*relieved*). Nothing like a nice cup of tea in bed.

SYLVIA (*smiling wanly*). Good night, Ethel—good night, Queenie. (*She moves down to the door.*)

QUEENIE. Good night, Aunt Sylvia.

ETHEL. Good night, Syl, sleep well.

SYLVIA (*going out*). I'm afraid there's not much hope of that !

(*She exits, closing the door.*)

ETHEL. Poor Sylvia, she's a bit of a trial sometimes.

QUEENIE. I don't know how you stand her, Mum.

ETHEL. She hasn't got anybody but us, you know. I wouldn't like to think of her living all by herself, she couldn't afford it anyhow.

QUEENIE (*moving towards the table*). She could if she did a bit of work. (*She sits in the chair* L. *of the table.*)

ETHEL. Well, she's tried once or twice, and it's never been any good. Remember when she answered that advertisement in nineteen twenty-three and got herself to Bexhill as a companion to Mrs. Philips ? Oh, dear ! (*She laughs.*)

QUEENIE (*also laughing*). She was home inside two weeks and in bed for four.

ETHEL. If it hadn't been for Bertie getting killed she'd have been all right, I expect.

QUEENIE. What was he like ?

ETHEL (*rising*). A bit soppy I always thought, but still she liked him.

QUEENIE. How awful to be so dependent on a man living or dying that it could ruin your whole life. I don't think I ever would be.

ETHEL (*packing up the supper things, above the table*). Well, don't be too sure. If your Dad had gone I wouldn't have been the woman I am to-day, far from it.

QUEENIE. You wouldn't have gone on moping about it always though, would you ?

ETHEL. I don't rightly know. My heart would have broke and I suppose I should have had to put it together again as best I could.

QUEENIE. Oh, Mum !

ETHEL (*picking up some plates*, C.). What is it ?

QUEENIE. You do make me feel awful sometimes.

ETHEL. Good 'eavens, child, why ? (*Putting down the plates.*)

QUEENIE. Oh, you just do.

ETHEL (*looking at her out of the corner of her eye*). Heard from Billy since he went ?

QUEENIE (*offhand*). Oh yes, just a postcard with a camel on it.

ETHEL. A camel ?

QUEENIE. Yes, his ship stopped somewhere where there was camels, and so he sent me a picture of one.

ETHEL. His poor mother misses him something dreadful. (*Reaching for things at the* L. *end of the table.*) We all miss him really, don't we ?

QUEENIE (*looking away*). Yes—I suppose we do.

(*There is the sound of the front-door bell.*)

ETHEL (*sharply*). There's the bell !

QUEENIE (*jumping up*). I'll go !

(*She runs into the hall, but* VI *has opened the door before her.   There is the sound of voices and* PHYLLIS BLAKE *comes in, followed by* VI *and* QUEENIE.)

PHYLLIS (*coming up to* R. *of* ETHEL).   Please forgive me for calling so late, Mrs. Gibbons, but I just popped over on mv bike to see if Reg had come back yet.

VI.   Well, he hasn't.   (*She crosses below the table to the fire.*)

(QUEENIE *goes to the* R. *end of the table.*)

ETHEL.   That's all right, dear, sit down and have a cup of tea.

PHYLLIS (*sitting above the table*).   Thanks very much, Mrs. Gibbons, I must be getting back in a minute.

ETHEL (*crossing above her to the* R. *end of the table*).   Time for one cup, anyway.   (*She sits, and pours it out.*)

QUEENIE (*moving to the* L. *end of the table*).   Dad's not back either, but he's due at any minute, him and Mr. Mitchell next door have been driving a bus.   (*She sits.*)

PHYLLIS.   Both of them ?

VI (*sitting on the* R. *arm of the armchair*).   Mr. Mitchell's the conductor.

PHYLLIS.   Have you heard from Reg, Mrs. Gibbons ?

ETHEL.   No, I'm afraid not, dear.   He's off somewhere with Sam Leadbitter and those men at that club they belong to—I don't know what they've been up to, I'm sure.

VI.   I went to Sam's bookshop in the Tottenham Court Road two days ago, the day Reg had a row with Dad and slammed out and said he wasn't coming back, and Sam said he was all right but he'd promised not to tell where he was until the strike was over.

QUEENIE.   Mother's afraid he might have got himself into trouble.

PHYLLIS.   He'll be all right, Mrs. Gibbons, don't you worry.

ETHEL.   I can't help it, I'm afraid.   You read in those nasty bits of newspaper they hand round, about there being riots and people being arrested and houses being burnt down and soldiers charging the crowds and all sorts of horrors . . .

QUEENIE.   You can't always believe what you read in the papers, even little ones.

VI.   If you ask me, I shouldn't think he's been doing anything at all but run around the streets hollering, that's all any of 'em seem to do.

ETHEL (*hopelessly*).   I wish he'd come back, whatever he's been doing.   I wish your dad hadn't gone at him like that.   I shan't have a moment's peace until I know he's safe.

VI.   I'm going to see that Sam Leadbitter again to-morrow morning first thing and if he won't tell me where Reg is I'll stand in the shop and yell until he does.

(*At this moment there is a great commotion outside in the garden*
All rise. FRANK *and* BOB'S *voices are heard singing* " *Rule*
Britannia " *at the top of their lungs.* *They come in* C., *from*
S.L., *grimy but gay.* BOB *is* R. *of* FRANK.)

FRANK (*striking an attitude just inside the french windows*).
. . . " Britons never, never, never shall be slaves ! "

ETHEL (*to above the* R. *end of the table*). 'Old your noise, Frank
Gibbons, you'll wake up the whole street.

FRANK (*coming down* L.C.). Who cares ! We have come
unscathed, my friend and I, through untold perils, and you
grumble about a bit of noise.

ETHEL. You've come unscathed through a few public-houses,
too, or I'm no judge.

BOB (*coming down* C.). Well, there's no denying, Mrs. G.,
we had a couple at the " Plough " with Captain Burchell, who
brought us all the way from Baker Street in his car, and then just
one more next door with me.

FRANK. That makes three all told, not so bad when you
come to think we've saved our country from the 'orrors of bloody
revolution.

ETHEL. And don't swear, neither.

FRANK. I was using the word in its literal sense, Ethel.

ETHEL. You'd better go and wash while I dish up your
supper. You'll stay and have a bite, won't you, Bob ?

BOB. No, thanks all the same. Nora's got something for me
next door.

FRANK. Have a drink ?

ETHEL. You've had quite enough drink, Frank, and well you
know it.

BOB. Better not, old man. Ethel's right,—the women
are always right. That's why we cherish them, isn't it,
Queenie ?

ETHEL. You'd better cherish yourself next door, Bob Mitchell.
Nora'll be having one of her upsets if she's got something hot
ready for you and you're not there to eat it.

BOB. All right, all right—I thought I'd just deliver your old
man safe and sound into your loving arms. Good night, all.

(*He turns to go.* FRANK *puts his hand on his arm.*)

FRANK. That's right, drive my best pal out of the house,
that's all the thanks he gets for saving my life.

ETHEL. How d'you mean, saving your life ?

FRANK. An old lady at Cricklewood attacked me with an
umbrella, and quick as a flash he wrested it from her and hit her
on the bottom with it !

VI (*down* L., *giggling*). Oh, Dad, you are awful !

FRANK. Good night, cock, see you to-morrow.

Bob. Righto, sweet dreams. (*He turns up to the window.*)
Toodle-ooo, everybody!

(*He exits through the french windows.*)

Ethel. Go on, Frank. (*She starts cutting some bread.*)
Here, Queenie, this bread's like iron, run into the kitchen and
make your dad a bit of toast while I get the soup; the toaster's
on the dresser.

(Queenie *rises, going below the table.*)

Queenie (*taking the bread and going out*). All right, Mum.

(Frank *goes out after her.*)

Vi (*crossing* r.). I'll get the soup, Mother, you stay here, you're
tired.

Phyllis. Can I help?

Ethel. No, thank you, dear.

(Vi *exits* r. Ethel *crosses above the table to* l.)

Phyllis. Mr. Gibbons and Mr. Mitchell were in the war
together, weren't they?

Ethel (*at the fireplace*). Yes, and to hear them talk you'd
think they were the only two that was.

(*There is the sound of the front-door bell.*)

Phyllis (*rising*). I'll go, Mrs. Gibbons.

(Phyllis *runs out of the room.* Ethel *stands by the fireplace
waiting anxiously. There is the sound of voices in the hall, then*
Sam *comes in holding* Reg *by the arm.* Phyllis *follows them.*
Reg's *head is bandaged.* Ethel *gives a cry.*)

Ethel (*moving in* l.c.). Reg! What's happened?

Sam (*bringing* Reg *across, below the table*). He's all right, Mrs.
Gibbons——

Ethel (*taking his arm*). Here, Reg, sit down here, dear.
(*She helps him to the chair* l. *of the table.*)

Reg (*sitting down*). Don't fuss, Mother, I'm all right.

Sam (*below the table, to* c.). There was some trouble in the
Whitechapel Road, and he got hit by a stone. That was yesterday. (*He breaks to* l.c.)

Ethel (*above* Reg's *chair*). What was he doing in the Whitechapel Road yesterday or any other time?

(Phyllis *has moved above the table to* r.c. Reg *sees her.*)

Reg (*smiling a little*). Hallo, Phyl, what are you doing here!

Phyllis. I came over on me bike to find out where you were.

Reg. Oh, I see . . . Thanks.

(Phyllis *sits at the* r. *end of the table.*)

ETHEL. I've been worrying my heart out about you; you ought to be ashamed of yourself.

(FRANK *comes in* R., *followed by* VI, *who carries a plate of soup.*)

FRANK. Hallo—what's up? (*He moves up,* R. *of the table.*)

ETHEL (*behind* REG). It's Reg, he's been hurt.

SAM (*down* L.C., *below the armchair*). It's nothing serious. I took him to the hospital last night, the doctor said it was only a graze.

VI (*above the table, at the* R. *end. Grimly*). This is all your fault, Sam. You know that, don't you? (*She puts down the plate of soup.*)

FRANK. Shut up a minute, Vi.

(VI *breaks to the sideboard.* FRANK *moves above the table to* R. *of* REG.)

Feel all right, son?

REG (*sullenly*). Of course I feel all right.

ETHEL. He'd better go up to bed, hadn't he?

FRANK. Leave him where he is a minute.

ETHEL. Don't go for him to-night, Frank, he looks worn out.

FRANK. I'm not going for anybody. I want my supper.

(*He goes to above the* R. *end of the table, and sits.* VI *comes down on his* R., *with a spoon and a napkin, and breaks up* C. ETHEL *sits on the table, above it, near the* L. *end, and holds* REG's *hand.* QUEENIE *enters with the toast and brings it round,* R. *of* FRANK.)

VI (*moving down* L.C., *above and* R. *of* SAM). You may not be going for anybody, Dad, but I am.

SAM (*crossing below the table to the door*). I think I'll be getting along now.

VI (*coming down* C. *below and to* L. *of* REG's *chair*). Not till you've heard what I've got to say, you're not.

(SAM *checks at the door.*)

REG. Oh, shut up, Vi, what's it got to do with you?

VI. It's all very fine for you to say that nothing serious has happened, Sam, but I should like to remark here and now that it's small thanks to you that it hasn't. Reg thinks you're wonderful, but I don't think you're wonderful. I'd think more of you if you did a bit more and talked a bit less. And the next time you come here on a Sunday evening and start pawing me about and saying that Love's the most glorious thing in the world for rich and poor alike, you'll get such a smack in the face that'll make you wish you'd never been born . . . (*She moves to below the centre of the table.*) You get out of this house once and for all and don't you show your nose in it again until you've

changed your way of thinking. Go on, get out ! I don't want
ever to see you again as long as I live !

(*In silence* SAM *turns and goes out of the room. VI waits until she
hears the front-door slam and then bursts into tears, turns* L.
and up C., *rushing out into the garden.* ETHEL *rises and moves
to up* L.C.)

FRANK. Where's the pepper got to ?

(QUEENIE *gets the pepper from the sideboard.*)

ETHEL. Oh, dear—I'd better go after her. (*She crosses up
to the windows.*)

FRANK. Much better leave her alone.

(ETHEL *hesitates at the windows, then turns back into the room.*)

REG. Vi hadn't any right to go at Sam like that. What
does she know about anything, anyway ?

FRANK. You keep quiet, son. I'll talk to you presently.

ETHEL (*moving to above the chair above the fire*). He really
ought to go to bed, Frank, he looks that seedy . . . (*To* REG.)
Is your head paining you, dear ?

REG (*irritably*). No, Mum, it's all right, just aching a bit, that's
all.

PHYLLIS (*rising*). I think I'd better be getting back now,
Mrs. Gibbons.

ETHEL. Very well, dear, be careful how you go, there's
probably a lot of people about to-night.

PHYLLIS (*breaking* R.). Good night, Queenie.

QUEENIE. Good night, Phyl.

PHYLLIS. Good night, Mr. Gibbons.

(ETHEL *moves above the armchair, down to the fire.*)

FRANK. Good night, Phyllis.

PHYLLIS (*looking across at* REG). I hope your head'll be better
in the morning, Reg.

REG. Thanks for coming round.

PHYLLIS. Good night.

REG (*looking at her*). See you to-morrow ?

PHYLLIS. Oh—all right.

(*She goes out* R.)

FRANK (*finishing his soup and toast*). Run out into the garden,
Queenie, and fetch Vi in, it's time we was all in bed.

QUEENIE (*going up* C.). Righto, Dad.

(*She goes into the garden.*)

FRANK (*pushing his plate aside*). Go on up, Ethel, I'll turn
out.

ETHEL (*crossing below the armchair to* L. *of the table*). Promise

me you won't be hard on him to-night, Frank—look, he's as
white as a sheet.

REG (*defiantly*). I feel fine, Mum, don't worry about me.

FRANK. Well, that's good news, anyway.

ETHEL. All right. (*She crosses to the door* L. *and turns to look
at* REG). Come in and say good night to me on your way to bed.

REG. All right.

(ETHEL *stands about helplessly for a moment, and then, after one
more imploring look at* FRANK, *she goes out of the room.* FRANK
*rises, crosses to the sideboard and takes a bottle of whisky, a
syphon and two glasses from it.*)

FRANK. Feel like a drink, Reg ? (*He brings the whisky, etc.,
to the table* R.C.)

REG (*surprised*). Oh—yes, thanks.

(FRANK *pours two drinks out in silence and takes one over to* REG.)

FRANK. Here you are.

REG (*taking it*). Thanks, Dad. (*He rises.*)

FRANK. Here goes. (*He drinks.*)

REG (*also drinking*). Here goes.

(FRANK *crosses to the chair above the fire.* QUEENIE *and* VI *come
in from the garden.* VI *is no longer crying.* She crosses
down* L.C.)

QUEENIE (*up* C.). Has Mum gone up ?

FRANK. Yes, a couple of minutes ago.

QUEENIE (*coming down* C.). Will you turn out ?

FRANK. Yes ; you might shut the windows though. Is
Percy in all right ?

QUEENIE (*turning back and shutting the windows*). Yes, he's
asleep in the kitchen.

VI. Good night, Dad.

FRANK (*kissing her*). Good night, old girl.

VI (*crossing down* R.). Good night, Reg.

(*She goes out.*)

QUEENIE (C., *looking at the table*). I suppose I'd better clear
these things.

FRANK. Leave them for Edie in the morning.

QUEENIE. All right. (*She crosses to* FRANK.) Good night
Dad.

FRANK (*kissing her*). Good night, Queenie.

QUEENIE (*crossing towards the door*). Good night, Reg. (*She
picks up her bag and cigarettes from the bamboo table.*)

REG. Good night.

(*Exit* QUEENIE, *closing the door.*)

Well, Dad—let's have it and get it over with.

FRANK. Easier said than done—you and me don't quite see things the same way, do we ?

REG. No, I suppose not. (*He moves down to the chair below the fire.*)

FRANK. That's the trouble really. It's a pity, too, and I don't see what there is to be done about it. Got any ideas ?

REG (*sitting down* L.). I'm not a kid any more, you know, Dad. I'm grown up now.

FRANK. Yes, I realize that all right. (*He breaks to* C.)

REG. I know you think all the things I believe in are wrong . . .

FRANK. That's where you make a mistake, son, I don't think any such thing. You've got a right to your opinions the same as I've got a right to mine. The only thing that worries me is that you should get it into your head that everybody's against you, and what's more, that all these ideas you've picked up from Sam and Sam's friends are new. They're not new, they're as old as the hills. Anybody with any sense has always known about the injustice of some people having a lot and other people having nothing at all, but where I think you go wrong is to blame it all on systems and governments. You've got to go deeper than that to find out the cause of most of the troubles of this world, and when you've had a good look, you'll see likely as not that good old human nature's at the bottom of the whole thing. (*He sips his whisky.*)

REG. If everybody had the same chance as everybody else, human nature'd be better, wouldn't it ?

FRANK. It doesn't seem as though we were ever going to find that out, does it ? It looks like a bit of a deadlock to me.

REG. As long as we go on admitting that, the workers of the world will go on being ground down and the capitalists will go on fattening on their blood and sweat.

FRANK (*moving to the table* R.C.). Oh, don't let's start all that now, let's use our own words, not other people's. (*He puts his glass on the table.*)

REG. I don't know what you mean.

FRANK (*moving to* L.C.). Oh, come off it, Reg, a kid of your age talking about blood and sweat and capitalism ! When I was rising twenty I had a damn sight more cheerful things to think about than that, I can tell you.

REG. Old people always think that all young people want is to enjoy themselves.

FRANK. Don't you sit there and tell me you 'aven't been enjoying yourself tip-top these last few days running about the streets and throwing stones and yelling your head off . . .

REG. It's no use talking, Dad, you don't understand, and you never will.

FRANK. No, you're quite right, arguing never got anybody

anywhere. (*He breaks* L., *to below the armchair*.) I'll just give you one bit of advice, and then we'll call it a day. How does that suit ?

REG (*suspiciously*). What is it ?

FRANK. It's this, son. I belong to a generation of men, most of which aren't here any more, and we all did the same thing for the same reason, no matter what we thought about politics. Now all that's over and we're all going on as best we can as though nothing had happened. But as a matter of fact several things did happen and one of them was the country suddenly got tired—it's tired now. But the old girl's got stamina and don't you make any mistake about it ; and it's up to us ordinary people to keep things steady. That's your job, my son, and just you remember it. And the next time you slam out of the house without a word and never let your mother know where you are and worry her to death, I'll lather the living daylight out of you. Now cut along upstairs and get a bit of sleep. (*He breaks to the fire*.)

REG (*rising*). All right, Dad. (*He crosses* R.)

FRANK. And don't forget to go in and say good night to your mum.

REG (*at the door*). All right, Dad. Thanks, Dad.

He exits, closing the door. FRANK *looks round the room, moves to the table, finishes his drink, turns out the lights and follows him as—*

The lighting fades and the CURTAIN *falls.*

ACT II

SCENE 1

TIME.—*October*, 1931. *It is about ten o'clock in the morning. The windows are shut, the curtains are open.*

FRANK *is alone in the room finishing his breakfast and reading the "Daily Mirror." He is sitting above the table. He has aged rather during the last six years. His hair is much thinner on the top and his eyes are not what they were, which necessitates his wearing glasses for reading. He is dressed in the trousers and waistcoat of a new pepper-and-salt suit, but no coat. He also has a wing collar and a grand grey silk tie, and carpet slippers. QUEENIE, wrapped in a Japanese silk kimono and with her hair done up in a net, rushes into the room, grabs her hand-bag off the mantelpiece and rushes out again. FRANK looks up, stirs his tea thoughtfully and goes on reading his paper. EDIE comes in with a tray, leaving the door open.*

During the ensuing scenes there are various sounds of commotion going on in the house. Scamperings up and down the stairs ; doors slamming ; bath-water running and occasional signs of altercation between members of the family.

EDIE (*to above the R. end of the table*). Mrs. Gibbons said I could clear now so as to give me time to go and dress.

FRANK. Righto, Edie, just leave me with me tea.

EDIE (*piling plates on to the tray*). That bath takes a terrible time to run out ; it's my belief the plug-hole's stopped up.

FRANK. Better pop round to the tobacconist's and telephone Mr. Freeman.

EDIE. I shan't 'ave time this morning.

FRANK. To-morrow'll do.

EDIE. Wasn't it awful about poor Mrs. Flint's dress ?

FRANK. What happened to it ?

EDIE. Percy's been curled up on it all night, covered it with 'airs, he 'as. She nearly 'ad a fit when she found 'im. Wonder you didn't 'ear the noise going on.

FRANK. The whole 'ouse has been in an uproar since eight o'clock.

EDIE. Well, we don't 'ave weddings every day of the week, do we ?

FRANK. No, thank God.

EDIE (*going out with the tray*). One thing, we've got a lovely day for it.

FRANK. That's right.

(*Exit* EDIE. FRANK, *left alone for a moment, goes on with his paper.* EDIE *returns.*)

Edie. D'you mind if I move your tea on to the sideboard a minute ? I'll 'ave to change the cloth.

Frank (*rising*). All right—I'll give you a hand. (*He places the teapot, milk-jug, sugar-basin and his cup on the sideboard and helps* Edie *to change the tablecloths during the ensuing few lines.*)

Edie (*during bus.*). I went with Mrs. Gibbons to the " Plough " last night to see the upstairs room. They've done it up lovely. We 'ad a look at the cake too, it's ever so pretty. Mrs. Gibbons says I can 'ave a bit to take 'ome to Ernie. Catch ! (*Throwing one end of the cloth at him.*)

(*They fold the cloth together.*)

Frank. Ernie must be getting quite a big boy now.

Edie. 'E's nearly sixteen, but you'd never think it—'e's short like Dad, you know.

Frank. Oh, I see.

Edie. 'E started trying to shave himself the other day with Dad's razor ; you'd have died laughing if you'd seen 'im.

Frank. Did he cut himself ?

Edie. Not badly, just took the top off one or two spots.

(Edie *goes out.* Frank *puts the tea-things back on the table and sits down again. Presently* Bob Mitchell *taps at the window.* Frank *gets up and lets him in.*)

Bob. Well, we've got a nice day for it. (*He comes down* L.C.)

Frank (*returning to the table*). Want a cup of tea ?

Bob. No, thanks—I'll have a Gold Flake though, if you've got one.

Frank. There's a packet on the mantelpiece ; chuck us one too while you're at it.

(Bob *goes to the mantelpiece, takes a cigarette himself and throws the packet over to* Frank, *who misses it.*)

Missed it ! Can't see a thing with these glasses.

Bob (*at the fire*). You'll get used to 'em. (*Crossing to* Frank *at the table, he lights* Frank's *cigarette and then his own.*)

Frank. How's Nora ?

Bob. A bit more cheerful—she always is when Billy's home. One thing, her legs don't pain her any more, she just hasn't got any feeling in 'em at all. The doctor says she won't get no worse nor no better either—just stay about the same.

Frank. Well, as long as she's a bit brighter in herself I suppose we mustn't grumble.

Bob. It was that last miscarriage six years ago that did her in, you know ; she'd probably have been all right if it hadn't been for that.

Frank. Poor old Nora.

Bob. Well, this is a nice conversation for us to be having

on the festive day, I will say.　How's the happy bridegroom ?

FRANK (*sitting above the table*).　The happy bridegroom locked himself in the bathroom for nearly an hour this morning ; you'd think he hadn't washed for a month.

BOB (*moving round chair* L. *of the table*).　Natural anxiety, old man—can't blame 'im !

FRANK.　Funny to think of starting off on an 'oneymoon, isn't it ?　Seems a hell of a long time ago since we did.

BOB (*sitting* L. *of the table* R.C.).　Where did you go for yours ?

FRANK.　Ramsgate, and it poured with rain without stopping all the time.

BOB.　We went to Swanage.　Nora had relatives near there ; it was awful.

FRANK.　Well, Reg and Phyl ought to enjoy themselves all right.　It'll be a change anyway going abroad for the first time.　I got them special rates all along the line.　Even old Baxter himself took a hand.

BOB.　Where are they stopping to-night ?

FRANK.　Dover.　Then they get the morning boat and they're in Nice first thing the next day.

BOB.　Pretty posh going to the South of France for your honeymoon, nest par ?

FRANK.　Oui, oui.

BOB.　You've held that job at Tickler's steady ever since the war, haven't you ?

FRANK.　Yes, but I nearly lost it once.

BOB.　How was that ?

FRANK.　Well, I'm all right on the business side, you know, travellers' cheques and letters of credit and what not, but once one of our young gentlemen downstairs smashed himself up in a car and I had to go behind the counter for a month—oh, dear !—Mr. Baxter sent for me to his office.　" Listen, Frank," he says, " there have been complaints.　You've issued no less than four sets of tickets to the wrong places inside of the last week through not being able to pronounce the foreign names properly !　And as we can't afford to have our customers losing themselves all over the Continent you'd better go back to your figures ! "　After that he engaged a couple of la-di-da young chaps with Oxford accents.　You should hear them !　I thought one of 'em had swallowed a fishbone the other day, but he was only saying " Marseilles " !

(SYLVIA *comes hurriedly into the room.　She is dressed in a very old wrapper and her head is swathed in a towel.　She sees* BOB, *gives a scream of horror and runs out again.　She speaks the ensuing dialogue through the half-open door.*)

SYLVIA.　Fancy me coming in looking like this in front of Mr. Mitchell !　What will he think ?

FRANK. Don't worry. He's broad-minded.

SYLVIA. I had my hair set yesterday and I didn't dare let the damp get to it while I was having my bath.

FRANK. What d'you want, anyway ?

SYLVIA. Mrs. Flint's feather-boa—she says it's in a box on the table by the fire—one of its tassels is loose.

FRANK (*rising*). Hold on a minute. (*Crossing* L., *he takes a box off the table above the fireplace.*) Is this it ? Marked "Fragile" ? (*He crosses below the table to the door* R.)

SYLVIA. Yes, that's it—thanks.

(FRANK *hands* SYLVIA *the box round the door. She goes.*)

FRANK (*shutting the door and coming back above the table*). This house has been a fair circus all the morning, I give you my word.

BOB. Reg is doing all right, isn't he, now ?

FRANK. Yes, he got his rise. He's assistant clerk to one of the managers.

BOB. No more of that Bolshie nonsense ?

FRANK (*sitting above the table*). Oh no, he's got quite a lot of horse sense, you know, underneath. He had a nice look at the Labour Government and saw what a mess they was making of everything. You should have heard him the other night when the election results come through—jumping up and down like a jack-in-the-box, he was. He's Britain for ever now, all right.

BOB. Well, that's good news.

FRANK. Sam shook him a bit too, you know, giving up that old Bombshell bookshop of his and marrying Vi and settling down. Oh yes, we've all gone back to being the backbone of the Empire.

(REG *enters in his shirt-sleeves. He carries two ties in his hand.*)

REG. Dad—— (*He sees* BOB.) Oh, hallo, Uncle Bob.

BOB. Hallo, Reg—feeling nervous ?

REG (*grinning*). My legs feel a bit funny. (*Moving up* R. *of the table.*) Is Billy nearly ready ?

BOB. Yes, and he's got the ring all right too. I saw him put it in his pocket myself. He'll be here in a minute.

REG. Which tie d'you think, Dad ? The bow, or the long one ?

FRANK. Let's have a look. (*He holds them both up.*) Very pretty colouring. Try the bow, it looks more dressy.

(REG *crosses* L.)

REG (*tying the bow in front of the glass on the mantelpiece*). Aunt Sylvia's been having a good cry upstairs.

FRANK. What about ?

REG. Oh, first of all, she said she felt seedy and that weddings always upset her anyhow, then Granny flew at her and said if only she'd had the sense to get married herself we should all have been saved a lot of trouble !

FRANK. I don't know how those two would get on without each other and that's a fact. (*He rises.*) You're doing that all wrong.

BOB (*rising*). I'll be getting along now and get myself spruced up for the happy moment.

FRANK. Righto.

BOB (*moving up to the window*). See you at the church, Reg.

REG. You might tell Billy to get a move on, Uncle Bob.

BOB. I will.

(*He exits* C. FRANK *goes to the door, opens it and looks out, closes it and looks at* REG.)

FRANK. Well, son ! (*Moving over to the table* R.C.)

REG (*finishing his bow*). Well, Dad !

FRANK. I suppose I ought to be giving you a few bits of fatherly advice by rights.

REG (*turning ; blandly*). What about, Dad ?

FRANK. Well, there's the facts of life, for instance.

REG. I could probably tell you a few things about them. (*He breaks a pace down stage.*)

FRANK (*moving to the chair above the fire*). I bet you could at that. (*There is a pause.*) Reg——

REG (*solemnly*). Yes, Dad ?

FRANK. And I'll trouble you to wipe that innocent look off your face before I say what I've got to say.

REG. What have you got to say, Dad ?

FRANK. That's right, make the whole thing easy for me.

REG. I don't know what you're talking about.

FRANK. I'm not talking about anything yet. Sit down.

REG. All right—fire away. (*He sits in the armchair down* L.)

FRANK (*sitting*). Now, Reg.

REG. Yes, Dad ?

FRANK (*with an effort*). Would you say—taken by and large—that you'd been a good boy on the whole—since you've grown up ?

REG. Depends what you mean by good.

FRANK. You know what I mean all right, so don't talk so soft.

REG. Women ?

FRANK. Yes.

REG. Oh, I've had my bits of fun every now and again.

FRANK. Never got yourself into any sort of trouble, have you, without telling me ?

REG. No, Dad.

Frank. Marriage is a little different, you know, from just— having a bit of fun.

Reg (*fidgeting*). Yes—I expect it is.

Frank. Women aren't all the same by any manner of means, some of them don't care what happens so long as they have a good time ; marriage isn't important to them beyond having the ring and being called Mrs. Whatever-it-is. But your mother wasn't that sort and I don't think Phyllis is, either. She's a nice girl and she loves you a lot.

Reg. I know, Dad.

Frank. And when a woman loves you that much she's liable to be a bit over-sensitive, you know. It's as well to remember that.

Reg. I'll remember, Dad.

Frank. Just go carefully with her—be gentle. You've got a long time to be together, all your lives, I hope. It's worth while to go easy and get to know each other gradual. And if later on, a long time later on, you ever get yourself caught up with someone else, just see to it that Phyllis doesn't get hurt by it. Put your wife first always. Lots of little things can happen on the side without doing much harm providing you don't make a fool of yourself and keep quiet about it. But anything that's liable to bust up your home and your life with your wife and children's not worth it. Just remember that and you won't go far wrong.

Reg. All right, Dad—thanks a lot.

Frank. I only hope you'll have as good a wife as I've had. I can't say more than that, can I ?

Reg. No, Dad.

Frank (*rising*). Well, I'd better be getting myself dressed up—so long, son.

(*He rather clumsily puts his arms round* Reg *for a minute and then goes out of the room.* Reg, *left alone, slowly crosses* c., *takes a cigarette out of the packet on the table, lights it and then returns to the glass above the fire and scrutinizes his face in it.* Billy *enters through the french window. He has grown matured and set with the years, and is now wearing the uniform of a Petty Officer.*)

Billy (*crossing down* c.). Don't worry, old man—you look gorgeous.

Reg (*turning*). Oh, it's you, is it ?

Billy. All ready for the ball and chain ?

Reg. You're too bloody cheerful by half.

Billy. Of course I am. I'm a sailor, aren't I ? All sailors are bright and breezy, it's in the regulations.

Reg. You must be the life and soul of your ship.

Billy. Oh, I am, I am. Only the other morning the Admiral

sent for me. "Mitchell," he said, "make me laugh!" So I told him the one about the parrot. "Mitchell," he said, "the ship's yours." "What'll I do with it?" I said. "Scuttle it," he said, and cut his throat from ear to ear.

REG. Have you got the ring all right?

BILLY. Well, as a matter of fact, I dropped it down the what's-it, but don't worry, we sent for a plumber.

REG (*crossing* R., *below the table*). I'd better go and get my coat, we'll have to be starting in a minute.

BILLY. Righto.

(REG *opens the door and bangs into* QUEENIE *coming in.* QUEENIE *is wearing a blue bridesmaid's dress and hat and is carrying a bunch of flowers.*)

QUEENIE. Why can't you look where you're going? (*Breaking a pace down stage.*) You nearly knocked me down.

REG. Sorry, old girl——

(*He exits.* QUEENIE *sees* BILLY.)

QUEENIE. Oh, it's you.

BILLY. Yes. (*He turns away to the fire.*)

QUEENIE (*crossing above the table*). Well, it's a nice day anyhow, isn't it? (*Up* L. *of the table.*)

BILLY. Fine.

(QUEENIE *puts her flowers on the table and crosses to* R. *of the armchair.*)

QUEENIE. You haven't said anything to Reg, have you? You haven't said anything to anyone?

BILLY. Of course not. (*He crosses to the table* R.C.)

QUEENIE. I'm awfully sorry about last night, Billy, really I am. (*She comes to the* L. *end of the table, and sits on it.*)

BILLY (*above* C. *of the table*). No need to be sorry, it's not your fault.

QUEENIE. When you've gone back, they'll all be asking me questions—I don't know what to say.

BILLY (*not looking at her*). Tell 'em the truth. I love you and asked you to marry me. You don't love me and said No. It's simple enough.

QUEENIE. It sounds horrid when you say it like that.

BILLY. No use pretending, is there?

QUEENIE. No, I suppose there isn't. I am sorry though all the same; you do believe that, don't you?

BILLY. Yes, I believe it all right.

QUEENIE. I never did say I would, did I? I mean I never let you think——

BILLY. I'm not blaming you, I told you that last night. I just can't help feeling a bit low—that's natural enough, isn't it?

Queenie (*rising and moving* l.c.). I suppose you won't write to me any more now, will you ?

Billy. You're a funny girl, I must say.

Queenie (*turning to face* Billy). I don't see anything so **very** funny about that.

Billy. You want everything, don't you ?

Queenie. It's unkind to talk like that.

Billy (*crossing to her,* c.). You know I love you more than anyone else and want to marry you, don't you ? You've always known that, anyway. You turn me down flat and then want me to go on writing to you. What shall I have to write about to you any more ? If you've taken the trouble to read my letters up to date you might remember they were mostly about the future, and what fun we were going to have when we were together. All that's gone now, hasn't it ? I'll send you a weather report every so often if you like. (*He breaks a little* r.)

Queenie. If you're going to turn nasty about it there's no use saying any more. (*She moves* l. *to the fireplace.*)

Billy. There's someone else, isn't there ?

Queenie (*not turning*). I don't know what you mean.

Billy. I mean what I say. You're in love with someone else, aren't you ?

Queenie (*facing him*). It's no business of yours if I am.

Billy. It's true, though, isn't it ?

Queenie (*moving towards him* c.). Now look here, Billy——

Billy. Why couldn't you have told me last night, or a long time ago. Don't you trust me ?

Queenie. You haven't got any right to ask me things like that.

Billy (*taking a pace nearer to her*). Listen here, Queenie. You've been the only girl I've cared a damn about for getting on seven years now. We haven't seen much of each other on account of me being away at sea, but you've known all the time that I was thinking of you and hoping that as the years went by you'd grow out of some of your highfalutin' ideas and think me good enough to be your husband. All that gives me the right to ask you anything I like——

Queenie. No, it doesn't.

Billy. Is there someone else or isn't there ?

Queenie. Yes, there is, if you must know. So there !

Billy. Are you going to marry him ?

Queenie. If you say a word about this to anyone I'll **never** speak to you again as long as I live. (*She turns away* l.)

Billy. Are you going to marry him ?

Queenie. No.

Billy. Why not ?

Queenie. That's my affair. (*She moves up* l. *of the armchair and round to the* r. *of it.*)

Billy. Is he married already ?

QUEENIE. I wish you'd leave me alone.

BILLY (*moving up*). Is he ?

QUEENIE. Yes, he is ! (*Sitting on the R. arm of the armchair.*)
Now are you satisfied ?

BILLY (*breaking away up C., behind the table*). Oh, Queenie,
you're an awful fool—I do wish you weren't.

QUEENIE. Who are you calling a fool ! People can't help
their feelings.

BILLY. No, but they can have enough sense not to let their
feelings get the better of them. What you're doing's wrong
whichever way you look at it. There's your mother and father
to start with, it'll break their hearts if ever they find out about
it. Then there's the man's wife whoever she is ; you're laying
up trouble there. (*Moving towards her.*) But most important
of all there's you. You won't get much out of it in the long run
and don't you fool yourself. You're not that kind of girl really,
whatever you may think. It looks to me as if you're on the way
to mucking things up all round for yourself and everyone else——
(*He turns down to the front of the table.*)

QUEENIE (*rising*). Thanks very much for the lecture.

BILLY (*moving R. to the door*). You're quite right. It's no
good me saying any more. I'll go up and talk to Reg. (*Turning
at the door.*) Good-bye and good luck.

(*He exits quickly.* QUEENIE *stands still for a moment looking after
him, biting her lip. She looks, just for a second, as though she
might be going to cry, then she tosses her head and, turning to the
glass, begins to fiddle about with her hat.* ETHEL *comes in, followed by* FRANK. ETHEL *is elaborately dressed in grey silk.*
FRANK *has enhanced the glory of his pepper-and-salt suit by the
addition of a large white buttonhole and some obviously new
boots.*)

ETHEL (*coming below the table to R.C.*). Vi and Sam ought to
be here by now—I wonder where they are. (*She sits on a chair
below the table.*)

FRANK (*down R., to* QUEENIE). Been talking to Billy ?

QUEENIE. Yes. He's upstairs with Reg.

(FRANK *feels his feet, and then goes up to above the table.*)

FRANK. These boots are giving me what-for all right. If
they're like this now, what are they going to be like by the
evening ? (*He takes his cup and saucer to the sideboard.*)

QUEENIE (*at the fire*). A couple of weddings in one year is a
bit too much of a good thing if you ask me.

FRANK (*returning to the table*). Well, here's hoping you get
off soon and make the third.

QUEENIE (*moving to R. of the armchair*). I wish you wouldn't
say things like that, Dad, it sounds so vulgar.

FRANK. Very sorry, I'm sure. (*He takes the teapot to the sideboard.*)

QUEENIE (*sitting on the* R. *arm of the armchair*). When I marry, if I ever do, it will be in a registry office anyway—all this commotion.

FRANK (*moving to above the* L. *end of the table*). Your mother wouldn't like that—would you, Ethel ? (*He picks up a cigarette.*)

ETHEL. I certainly would not.

QUEENIE. I shouldn't let you know. I shouldn't let anybody know. I'd do it on the quiet. I don't like to think of everyone staring at me and making remarks.

ETHEL. I never heard such nonsense.

FRANK. Our Queenie has ideas of her own, Ethel, or anyway she thinks they're her own.

QUEENIE. I'll never be a bridesmaid again, anyhow, as long as I live—look at this dress—and the hat.

ETHEL (*rising, and crossing to the fireplace*). You've done something to it, haven't you ?

QUEENIE. You bet I have. (*Adjusting her hat.*) I wouldn't have worn it as it was.

ETHEL. You'll look different from all the others.

QUEENIE (*looking at* ETHEL). So I should hope.

ETHEL. Marjorie will be upset. She and Phyl took such a lot of trouble——

QUEENIE. They don't know anything about clothes, either of them. Thank Heaven none of the girls at the shop can see me looking such a sight.

FRANK (*moving round below the table to* R.). It seems to me they must be a pretty fancy lot, them girls at your shop ! We're always being told what they like and what they don't like. (*He sits at the* R. *end of the table.*)

QUEENIE. All right, Dad, there's no need for you to be sarcastic.

ETHEL. Don't snap at your father, Queenie. I don't know what's come over you lately.

QUEENIE (*with an edge on her voice*). Nothing's come over me —I just don't like looking common.

FRANK. I shouldn't worry about that if I was you—it can't be helped. After all, according to some people's standards I suppose you are common.

ETHEL (*crossing* R., *to above the table*). Frank, how can you say such a thing ! She's nothing of the sort. (*She sits.*)

FRANK. It's your mother's fault really, you know. She caught me on the 'op ! I was all set to marry a duchess when along she come and busted up the whole thing with her fatal charm. And what's more, the duchess never forgave me. That's why I haven't set foot inside Buckingham Palace these last thirty years.

QUEENIE. You think you're very funny, don't you, Dad ?

FRANK. I think you're the one that's funny, if you must know.

QUEENIE. Why, what have I done ?

FRANK. It isn't what you've done, my girl, it's what you're trying to do.

QUEENIE. And what's that, may I ask ?

FRANK. You're trying to be something you're not. There's nothing funnier than that. To see you flouncing about and putting on airs just because you happen to have polished Lady Kiss-me-quick's nails is enough to make a cat laugh.

QUEENIE (*rising, angrily*). You don't believe in people trying to better themselves, do you ? (*Moving to* L. *of the table.*) Just because you're content to stick in the same place all your life and do your bit of gardening on Saturday afternoons in your shirt-sleeves——

ETHEL. Don't you dare speak to your father like that !

QUEENIE. Living in a suburb and doing your own cooking and washing up may be good enough for you, but it isn't good enough for me. I'm sick of this house and everybody in it, (*she breaks up* C. *and turns*) and I'm not going to stand it much longer, you see——

ETHEL (*rising*). You're a wicked, ungrateful girl and you ought to be ashamed of yourself.

QUEENIE (*turning away up* L.C., *then down to the fire* L.). Well, I'm not, so there !

ETHEL. If it wasn't for being Reg's wedding day I'd lock you in your room till you came to your senses.

FRANK. Well, a few years ago we had Reg nagging at us because we were living on the fat of the land while the poor workers was starving. Now we have Queenie turning on us because we're not grand enough for her. I don't know what's wrong with our children, Ethel, my girl. Seems to me Vi's the only one who's got any real sense.

(ETHEL *sits again on the chair above the table.*)

QUEENIE. Vi ! Vi's different from me—can't you see—she always has been ! She doesn't like the things I like or want the things I want. She's perfectly happy in that mangy little flat doing her own housework and making her own clothes. She likes bossing Sam too. Why, he's a changed man since he married her.

ETHEL. So I should hope.

QUEENIE. It seems to me that all the spirit's gone out of him. He's just like anybody else now—just respectable.

FRANK. Well, what's the matter with that ?

QUEENIE. Oh, nothing. What's the use of arguing ! don't understand what I'm talking about.

FRANK (*rising*).   Don't waste your breath on us then, Queenie. (*Crossing below the table to* C. *as he speaks.*)   We're as we are and that's how we're going to stay, and if you don't like it you can lump it.   (*He turns at up* L.C. *to face* QUEENIE.)   One of these days when you know a bit more, you'll find out that there are worse things than being ordinary and respectable and living the way you've been brought up to live.   In the meantime—as long as you're with us, I mean—your Mum and me'd be much obliged if you'd keep your tongue between your teeth and behave yourself.   (*Moving* R., *above the table, to the* R. *end of it.*)   Now you'd better go upstairs, slap some more paint on your face, make yourself look as much like a tart as possible and do the girls at the shop credit.   (*Facing* QUEENIE *from* R.)   Go on—'op it !

(QUEENIE *flounces across* R., *and out of the room, slamming the door.*)

ETHEL.   There now.   She'll be snapping our heads off for the rest of the day.

FRANK (*breaking down stage*, R. *of the table*).   We spoilt her when she was little.   We've always spoilt her.

ETHEL.   No, Frank, it isn't only that.   She's upset about something—sort of strung up, she has been for a long time. (*Rising.*)   I wish I knew what it was.   (*She moves to* L.C.   *She looks at herself in the mantel mirror, from* L.C.)

FRANK.   You mean you think she's in some sort of trouble ?

ETHEL (*turning*).   I don't know what to think.   (*Moving down* C., *below the* L. *end of the table.*)   When Billy came back last year and they went out together nearly every evening, I thought everything was going to be all right, then they had words, I don't know what about I'm sure, and off he went.

FRANK.   Don't worry, old girl, it'll all come out in the wash.

(EDIE, *resplendent in a green dress and hat, rushes in.*)

EDIE.   The car's come.   It looks ever so nice all done up with white ribbons.

FRANK.   Good !   Let's have a look, Ethel.   You'd better call Reg, Edie—tell him it's here.

(EDIE *runs out.*   FRANK *and* ETHEL *go out into the hall and apparently open the front door, because they can be heard making exclamations of approval of the car.*   REG *and* BILLY *come clattering down the stairs and into the room.*   REG *is palpably nervous.*   BILLY *enters first and crosses to the fire.*)

REG (*checking at* C.).   I suppose we ought to be starting, oughtn't we ?

BILLY (*as he crosses to the fire*).   Yes, it's about time now ; it wouldn't do for the blushing bride to get there before we do.

(REG *moves up to* R. *of the armchair.* FRANK *and* ETHEL *return.* FRANK *remains down* R.)

ETHEL (*moving to* L. *of the table*).   Have you seen the car ? Mr. Stevens has done it up lovely !

REG.   Yes, we saw it drive up.

FRANK.   Feeling nervous, son ?

REG.   Yes, a bit.

ETHEL (*emotionally*).   Oh, Reg !   (*Sitting on the chair* L. *of the table.*)

REG (*crossing to her*).   Cheer up, Mother.

ETHEL (*fumbling for her handkerchief*).   I can't hardly believe it—it seems only the other day that——

REG (*putting his arm round her*).   All right, Mum, we know all about that.   I was a little toddler cutting me first teeth, and look at me now, a great grown man——

FRANK (*moving up above the* R. *end of the table*).   Don't start getting weepy now, Ethel, it's a wedding, not a funeral !

ETHEL.   Oh, hold your noise, Frank, and be quiet.

REG (*kissing her*).   See you at the church, Mum.   Cheero, Dad.   Come on, Billy.   (*He crosses* R., *below the table.*)

FRANK.   Cheero, son—don't forget to send the car straight back.

BILLY (*following* REG *to* R.).   I'll see to that—it'll be back in five minutes.

ETHEL.   Have you said good-bye to your Grannie and Auntie Syl ?

REG (*at the door*).   Yes—I saw them upstairs.

BILLY (*sternly*).   Come *on* !

REG.   All right.   Good-bye, all——

(REG *and* BILLY *exit* R.)

FRANK (*seeing that* ETHEL *is tearful*).   Come off it, Ethel, there's nothing to cry about.

ETHEL.   I can't help it.

FRANK (*to below the table*).   You'll make your nose red.

ETHEL.   I don't care if I do.   He's our only son, isn't he ? And he's going away from us, isn't he ?   That's enough to make any woman cry.

FRANK.   Well, they'll be back from the honeymoon in two weeks and living just round the corner——

ETHEL.   It's all very fine for you—you didn't bring him into the world and hold him at your breast——

FRANK.   I should have looked a proper fool if I had.   (*He turns up* R.)

(ETHEL *crosses to the mantel and looks in the glass.* FRANK *moves up and down between the sideboard and the table.* SYLVIA *comes in, leading* MRS. FLINT *by the arm.* SYLVIA *is wearing an artistic confection of brown and orange, also a necklace of thick amber beads.* MRS. FLINT *is in purple satin and a black flowered hat. She goes to the chair below the fire.*)

MRS. FLINT. If I could lay my hands on that cat I'd kill it. Half an hour it took me to pick the hairs off and the front of the skirt all creased too.

SYLVIA (*who has stopped* L.C.). It doesn't show.

MRS. FLINT (*looking balefully at* SYLVIA, *and sitting in the armchair*). Is that the new hat we've heard such a lot about ?

SYLVIA (*to below the chair*, L. *of the table*). Yes, it is.

MRS. FLINT (*grunting*). Oh !

SYLVIA (*turning*). Why ? Is there anything the matter with it ?

ETHEL (*peaceably, crossing to up* C.). I think it's very nice, don't you, Frank ?

FRANK (*above the table*). It looks fine—from here. (*He sits on the table.*)

MRS. FLINT. There's something a bit funny about the crown, isn't there ?

SYLVIA. I don't know what you mean. (*She goes to the mantel, looking in the glass.*)

MRS. FLINT. Well, of course, if you're satisfied.

ETHEL. Do be quiet, Mother. Don't take any notice of her, Sylvia.

MRS. FLINT. That'll be no change.

(SYLVIA *sits in the chair above the fireplace.* VI *and* SAM *come in.* QUEENIE *follows them.* SAM *has improved with the years. He is neatly dressed and wears an air of respectability which was lacking before.* VI *looks very assured and smart in a pink dress and hat.*)

VI (*crossing above the table to* ETHEL). The front door was open, so we came straight in.

ETHEL (*kissing her, meeting her up* R.C.). Why, Vi, how pretty you look, dear.

(VI *crosses* ETHEL *to* L.C.)

VI (*showing off her dress*). I only finished it at eleven o'clock last night.

(ETHEL *breaks a little towards* VI, *up* L.C.)

SAM (*up* R. *of the table*). The whole flat's been covered in paper patterns and bits of stuff and pins for the last ten days. (*He breaks to* R. *of* FRANK, *who stands.*) Has Reg gone ?

FRANK. Yes, he and Billy went about two minutes ago. They're sending the car straight back.

QUEENIE (*above the table, at the* R. *end*). I hope they'll get a move on. I've got to be on time to meet Marjorie and Doreen and Amy Weaver.

(ETHEL *moves to the fireplace*.)

VI. It does look nice, that dress, doesn't it, Sam ?

SAM. Very nice indeed.

QUEENIE. I think it's awful. (*She breaks a little* R. *of the table*.)

VI. Oh, you always say that, Queenie, it was exactly the same at my wedding.

(BOB MITCHELL *comes in through the french window, to* R. *of* ETHEL *and* VI.)

BOB. Hallo, Vi—hallo, Sam. Car come back yet ?

ETHEL. Tell Edie to keep an eye out for it, Queenie.

QUEENIE (*down* R., *calling to* EDIE). Edie—keep a look-out for the car—you'd better stay by the front-room window.

EDIE (*off*). All right.

MRS. FLINT. On my wedding day there was a thunderstorm and a man got struck by lightning just opposite the church.

FRANK. That must have cheered things up.

MRS. FLINT. One side of his face was all twisted.

QUEENIE. Why, Granny, did you stop in the middle of the service and pop out to have a look ?

MRS. FLINT. We did not, and I'll thank you, miss, not to be saucy.

QUEENIE. Saucy indeed—what a way to talk.

FRANK. I'm surprised at you, Mother, I am really, using such expressions in front of our Queenie. You know she meets all the best people nowadays.

QUEENIE (*moving up* R.). Oh, shut up, Dad.

(*A pause.*)

FRANK. Better sit down, hadn't we, all of us ?

(SAM *sits* R. *of the table*.)

No sense in standing about.

(*He goes down and sits in the chair below the door.* VI *sits above the table,* L. *end.* QUEENIE *in the chair* R. *of the whatnot, up* R. BOB *is on the arm of the settee up* L.)

ETHEL (*looking at the clock*). It ought to be back by now. (*She moves to the* L. *end of the table*.)

FRANK. Don't fuss, Ethel.

MRS. FLINT (*reminiscently*). It seems only yesterday.

ETHEL. What does, Mother ? (*She sits in the chair* L. *of the table*.)

MRS. FLINT. The day you and Frank was married. I can see your poor Aunt Connie now coughing her heart out in the vestry. It was only three months after that she was taken.

FRANK (*cheerfully*). That's right. That's right.

MRS. FLINT. I'll be lucky if I last out another year.

FRANK. On with the bloody motley.

MRS. FLINT (*darkly*). I don't suppose anybody'd mind much—there's many as might say it was a blessing in disguise, I shouldn't wonder.

FRANK. Now then, Mother—none of that.

MRS. FLINT. Doctor Spearman said my heart was thoroughly worn out ever since that bronchitis I 'ad in February.

SYLVIA (*still in the armchair above the fire—contemptuously*). Doctor Spearman !

MRS. FLINT. He's a better man than your Doctor Lewis any day of the week. If it hadn't been for him having presence of mind Mrs. Spooner would be dead as a door-nail at this very minute.

SYLVIA. That's what you say.

MRS. FLINT. Eleven o'clock she was doing her shopping and she was putting the joint in the oven at twelve—a nice bit of leg of lamb it was too, and at half-past one she was in the 'ospital lying flat on 'er back on the operating table—and if it hadn't been for Doctor Spearman——

ETHEL. I wonder what's happened to that car—it's getting on, you know.

BOB (*rising*). Shall I go out and have a look ?

FRANK. No——

(BOB *sits again.*)

Edie's watching out for it.

ETHEL. I suppose Billy remembered to tell the driver all right. He's a new man you know, not the same one we had for Vi's wedding. He might not have understood.

FRANK. Well, if it comes to the pinch we can walk, anyway, can't we ? It's only just up the road.

SAM. Vi oughtn't to do much walking.

VI. Don't be silly, Sam. It's months away yet.

SAM. All the same, it's silly to go taking risks.

FRANK (*at the door, shouting*). Any signs yet, Edie ?

EDIE. No——

(*She appears.*)

Mrs. Baker and Miss Whitney just come out of number twelve—you should see 'em—got up to kill, they are.

SYLVIA. That Miss Whitney—stuck-up thing !

ETHEL. Well, she'll have to sit next to Mr. Bolton at the table whether she likes it or not.

FRANK. Better got back to the front-room, Edie.

QUEENIE. Don't hang out of the window though, it looks silly.

EDIE (*reproachfully*). As if I would !

(*She goes.*)

SYLVIA. I had those pains again in the night, Ethel, something terrible they were—started about two o'clock.

MRS. FLINT. It's all those sweets you eat. There's nothing like sweets for giving you wind.

SYLVIA. It was *not* wind !

QUEENIE. It's nearly ten to—I think I'd better go on in a minute.

FRANK. I wish everybody'd stop fussing, it gives me the pip.

ETHEL. It shouldn't have taken Reg and Billy more than three or four minutes to get there.

MRS. FLINT. I'm sure I hope nothing dreadful's happened to them.

VI. Oh, Granny, what could have ?

MRS. FLINT. Accidents will happen.

QUEENIE. Well, they can't have been struck by lightning, anyhow.

SYLVIA. I shouldn't think there was the chance of many accidents just between here and St. Michael's.

MRS. FLINT. Well, you never know.

FRANK (*irritably*). All right, all right. There's been a terrible accident, the wedding's off. Reg 'as got concussion and we're all going to spend the rest of the day yelling our eyes out ! How's that ?

SYLVIA. Some people seem to think of nothing but horrors ; it's morbid, that's what it is.

MRS. FLINT. I'll thank you not to call me names, Sylvia Gibbons.

SYLVIA. You make me tired.

ETHEL. Don't answer back, Sylvia, it'll only mean a row.

SYLVIA. I'm sure I don't want to say anything to anybody, but really——

MRS. FLINT. Pity you don't keep quiet, then !

SYLVIA (*losing her temper*). Who are you to talk to me like that—I've had about enough of your nagging——

FRANK. Shut *up*, Sylvia.

VI. You know it's no good arguing with her, Auntie Syl.

SYLVIA (*violently*). I don't know any such thing. (*Rising, to* L.C.) I tell you I'm sick of it—morning, noon and night it's the same thing—she's at me all the time, and I won't stand it. I've got as much right to be in this house as she has, just because she's old and pretends her heart's weak she thinks she can say what she likes, but I'll tell you one thing here and now, and that is that I've had enough trouble and sorrow and suffering in my life to put up with her eternal nagging and nasty insinuations. She's nothing but a spiteful, mischief-making old cat, and if I have any more of it, old as she is, I'll slap her face till her teeth rattle !

(*She bursts into violent hysterical tears.* MRS. FLINT, *with a cry of rage, struggles up from her chair.* FRANK *crosses* L. *and endeavours to calm her.* BOB, ETHEL *and* VI *and* SAM *help* SYLVIA, *who is sobbing, to* C. QUEENIE *regards the proceedings with obvious contempt. Everybody talks at once.* EDIE *rushes in from the hall.*)

EDIE (*excitedly, above the din*). It's here—it's here ! The car's here !

(*She exits.* FRANK *is down* L., *pacifying* MRS. FLINT. *The others are doing the same with* SYLVIA, *who is now sitting in the upper armchair. The general noise and* SYLVIA'S *sobs subside. All straighten themselves.*)

FRANK (*quietly*). Come on, Mother—it's time to go to the church.

(VI *comes down on the* R. *of* MRS. FLINT.)

VI. Come on, Granny—come with me. (*She leads* MRS. FLINT *across to the door, walking on her upstage side.*)
MRS. FLINT. I'm all right.
VI (*coaxingly*). You'd better, dear, you know what you are and it's quite a long service——
FRANK. Take her to the outside one, Vi, there's no need to trail all the way upstairs.

(VI *leads* MRS. FLINT, *still protesting, out of the room.* BOB, *taking her right arm, goes out with* SYLVIA, *who is making gallant efforts to control herself.* SAM *and* QUEENIE *follow them,* QUEENIE *walking above him.*)

(*Looks at* ETHEL *and laughs, then he slips his arm through hers—as they go.*) Come on, old girl——

The lights fade and the CURTAIN *falls.*

SCENE 2

TIME.—*November, 1931. It is about midnight.*
The room is empty and the door into the hall open. The stage is dark except for a glow from the dying fire. The french windows are closed and the curtains drawn over.

Presently QUEENIE *can be seen tiptoeing down the stairs. She is wearing a hat and coat and carrying a small suitcase. She puts*

*this down, just inside the door, switches on the light, goes, still
on tiptoe, over to the fireplace and props a letter up on the mantelpiece. Then, with a hurried look round, she switches off the light
again and goes out into the hall, taking her suitcase with her.
The front door is heard to open and close softly.*

*There is a slight pause. The clock on the mantelpiece strikes
twelve. There is a scuffling noise at the window, it opens and
the curtains blow out in the draught.* BOB'S *voice is heard to say
" Oh, dear ! " He comes in, followed by* FRANK. *They are
both in ordinary suits but wearing their war medals. They are
also both a little bit drunk.*

FRANK. God help poor sailors on a night like this !

BOB. Where's the light ?

FRANK (*fastening the window*). Over by the door.

(BOB *crosses above the table to the door* R.)

Lucky this was open, we'd have woke up Ethel if we'd of come in
by the front.

BOB (*switching on the light below the door* R.). 'Ere we
are.

FRANK (*above the* L. *end of the table*). Better shut that door
while you're at it. (*Taking off his raincoat.*)

BOB. Righto. (*He does so.*)

FRANK (*putting his raincoat on the back of the chair*). Now then.
(*He moves* R., *to the sideboard.*)

BOB (*crossing* L.C., *below the table*). Now then what ?

FRANK (*at the sideboard*). One more nightcap. (*He opens the
cupboard.*)

BOB (*taking off his raincoat*). You won't half have a thick head
in the morning ! (*He puts the coat on the settee up* L.)

FRANK (*producing whisky and glasses*). What about you ?

BOB. I'm past caring, old man.

FRANK. That's right—say when—— (*He pours out the
whisky.*)

BOB. Here, go easy—— (*Crossing above the table to the
sideboard.*)

FRANK (*handing* BOB *a glass*). 'Old it while I put the soda in.

BOB (*taking the glass*). Your eyes look terrible ! All swimmy.

FRANK. Never you mind about my eyes—yours don't look
so good from here ! (*He squirts the syphon violently, splashing
them both.*)

BOB. Look out !

FRANK. Oh dear ! Now I've wetted me Victoria Cross.

BOB. Don't you wish you had one.

FRANK. Fat lot of good it'd do me if I 'ad. (*The pouring out
of the drinks having been accomplished, he moves to* R. *of the table,
holding up his glass.* R.C.) I would like to take this auspicious

opportunity of saying that my old regiment's the finest in the world.

Bob (*crossing* c., *above the table*). Next to the East Surreys it is.

Frank. Here's to the Buffs! (*He drinks, crossing below the table to* r. *of* Bob c.)

Bob. Here's to the East Surreys!

Frank (*affectionately*). Bob, the East Surreys is the finest regiment in the world too——

Bob. That's right. (*To* l. *of the table.*)

Frank (*drinking*). Here's to the East Surreys!

Bob (*drinking*). Here's to the Buffs! (*He moves to* r. *of the armchair above the fire.*)

Frank (*moving to below the* l. *end of the table*). What was that one that chap told us about the couple in the park?

Bob (*sitting on the* r. *arm of the chair*). You mean the one when the copper comes up and starts arguing and the woman says——

Frank (*moving* l.c., *to* r. *of* Bob). No, no, no, not that one——

Bob. You don't mean the one the little bald bloke with glasses told us?

Frank. No, no, no—that was the one about the woman in the bath when the 'ouse caught on fire—bloody funny it was too, I will say—— (*He starts to laugh.*)

Bob. Oh, shut up, you'll start me off. (*He laughs.*)

Frank (*wiping his eyes*). That little bastard can tell 'em all right and no mistake about it——

Bob (*convulsed*). It wasn't what he said so much as the way he said it—dry, you know, that's what he was—dry——

Frank. That reminds me—— (*Crossing above the table to the sideboard* r.)

Bob (*following him*). Here, 'old on, old cock—I got to get home——

Frank (*turning to him*). I'll see you home, and then, and then we'll have one more with you.

Bob (r.c.). I suppose there's nothing to eat, is there?

Frank (*pouring fresh drinks and putting them on the table*). 'Ave a look in the sideboard.

(Bob *goes to the sideboard.*)

Bob. There's a barrel of biscuits. (*He gets out a barrel of biscuits.*)

Frank. There ought to be some fish-paste by rights. (*He joins* Bob *at the sideboard.*)

(Bob *brings the biscuits to the table.*)

(*Getting out a pot of paste and a bottle of O.K. sauce.*) The butter's in the larder so we'd better do without it—Sylvia sleeps just over the kitchen and she's got ears like a hawk. We've got to organize. (*He goes to the table, R. of* BOB.) We can spread the paste on the biscuits and put a bit of O.K. on top to pep it up.

BOB. It ought to sit nicely on that dinner we had ! Where's a knife——

FRANK (*to the R. end of the table*). In the drawer.

(*He belches. They both bow to each other.*)

Better out than in, that I will say.

(BOB *finds a knife in the drawer and brings it to the table.*)

BOB (*holding up his glass*). Huntley and Palmer ! (*He drinks.*)

FRANK (*holding up his glass*). Crosse and Blackwell—God bless 'em ! (*He drinks and sits on the chair above the table.*)

BOB (*giggling*). We shan't half look silly if Ethel catches us. (*Sitting L. of the table.*)

FRANK. It's me own house, isn't it ? I can do what I like in it. An Englishman's home is his castle.

BOB (*proffering him the bloater paste*). Here, smell that a minute.

FRANK. What's the matter with it ?

BOB. Seems a bit off to me.

FRANK (*smelling it*). No—don't be so fancy—it's only the rubber round the top. (*A pause.*) Heard from Billy lately ?

BOB. Yes—he writes once a week—he's in Malta now.

FRANK. Good old Billy ! He's a fine boy.

BOB. You know, I've never said much about it but I always thought that maybe Billy and Queenie might—one day——

FRANK. Oh, Queenie gives me a headache—all her airs and graces—a good hiding is what she needs.

BOB. That wouldn't be any use—some girls get like that—no doing anything with them.

FRANK (*patting* BOB's *arm affectionately*). Listen, Bob, old man. I want exactly what you want, see ? I've wanted Queenie and Billy to get together ever since they were kids. I'd rather have Billy in the family than anyone else in the world, and that's a fact—you know that, don't you ?

BOB. Of course I do.

FRANK. But it's no use trying to drive people the way they don't want to go.

BOB. I think Billy'd stand by her always, whatever she did.

FRANK (*almost sharply*). How d'you mean ?

BOB. I don't know—I just mean he loves her, that's all.

FRANK. Funny, isn't it, about having children and seeing what they grow up like.

BOB. Reg is the one for my money.

Frank (*smiling*). Now you're talking——

(*They sit in silence for a moment looking back over the years.*)

Bob. Well, it's a strange world and no mistake. I was thinking that to-night, looking at all those chaps in your regiment—wondering what they were feeling like—some of 'em looked all right, of course, but some looked a bit under the weather.

Frank. We've been lucky.

Bob. You've said it.

Frank (*rising and crossing to* l.c.). I wonder when the next war'll be. (*He breaks a little up* l.c.)

Bob. Not in our time, nor in our sons' time, thank God!

Frank (*turns down to above the* l. *end of the table*). I wouldn't bank on that.

Bob (*pushing his chair back a little*). How could there be? Everybody's disarming.

Frank (*above and to* r. *of* Bob). We are.

Bob. There's the good old League of Nations.

Frank. It don't seem able to have stopped Japan turning nasty.

Bob. Japan! Who cares about Japan? It's a nice long way off for one thing.

Frank (*breaking a pace* r.). Lots of trouble can start from a long way off.

Bob. Oh, don't you worry your head about Japan.

Frank (*thoughtfully*). Of course, I know if they really start behaving badly, all we got to do is to send a couple of battleships along and scare the little sods out of their wits.

Bob. That's right.

Frank. All the same——

Bob (*rising and moving to* l. *of* Frank). We've got the finest Navy in the world and don't you forget it.

Frank. As long as we treat it right.

Bob. How d'you mean?

Frank. What about Invergorden?

Bob. That wasn't the Navy's fault.

Frank. I never said it was.

Bob. Well then!

Frank. It was the fault of the old men at the top. It always is the fault of the old men at the top. They're the ones that muck things up. We can't afford to have much more of that sort of thing, you know.

Bob. Well, we got a nice new government now and everything in the garden's lovely.

Frank (*raising his glass*). Here's hoping! Stanley Baldwin!

Bob. Ramsay MacDonald! Well, I'll have to be pushing off home in a minute. (*He puts down his glass and goes to the* l. *end of the table.*)

FRANK (*taking* BOB's *glass*). Have one more before you go.

BOB (*to above the table*). Now listen, Frankie-boy—we're up to the gills already.

FRANK (*crossing to the sideboard*). Just a little one for the road.

BOB. The road ? I only got about three yards to go.

FRANK (*pouring whisky*). We don't have a binge like this every day of the week.

BOB (*making a dive at him*). Here, that's enough ! (*He catches* FRANK'S *arm to prevent him pouring out too much, causing him to drop the bottle on the floor with a crash.*)

FRANK (*as* BOB *backs a step*). Now you've done it ! We'll blame that on to poor old Percy. (*He picks up the bottle, then straightens up, suddenly.*) Quiet a minute—listen !

(*They both listen. There is the sound of footsteps on the stairs.*)

BOB. Here—I'd better 'op it. (*Turning up to the window.*)

FRANK (*to* R.C.). That's right, leave your best pal to face the barrage alone.

BOB (*returning, down* C.). Come on, pull yourself together— we're for it.

FRANK. Chest out—chin up !

(*They are standing rigidly to attention when* ETHEL *comes into the room. They salute. She is wearing a dressing-gown and her hair is in curlers.*)

ETHEL. And what d'you think you're doing, if I may make so bold ? (*She shuts the door after her and stands with her back to it.*)

FRANK. Bob was just going home.

ETHEL. Oh ! Just going home, was he ?

BOB. Sorry we woke you up, Ethel.

ETHEL. What was that you dropped ?

FRANK. The poor old John Haig.

ETHEL. I suppose you know what the time is, don't you ?

FRANK. Time was meant for slaves !

ETHEL. You go up to bed, Frank Gibbons, I'll have something to say to you later.

BOB. It was my fault, Ethel——

ETHEL. You ought to be ashamed of yourselves, both of you —men of your age—coming home drunk and waking up the whole house.

FRANK (*moving down to her between the sideboard and the table*). You're not a whole house, Ethel, old girl—you're just —just a little bungalow—for better or for worse—— (*He giggles.*)

ETHEL. I'll give you bungalow ! Go on, Bob, it's time you went home.

FRANK. Don't be hard on him, Ethel—he's my pal—he may

be looking a bit silly now, I'll admit—but he's my pal all the same.

BOB. Who's looking silly?

FRANK. You are!

BOB. What about you?

ETHEL. You both look silly—but it's nothing to what you're going to look in the morning. Go on, Bob. I'm not going to stand here much longer catching me death.

BOB (*getting his raincoat from the settee up* L.). All right—I can take a hint. Good night, Mrs. G. Good night, Sergeant. It's been a pleasure. (*To* FRANK.) Steady, the Buffs!

(*They ad lib. here:* " Black Watch," " Sherwood Foresters," " East Surreys," " Royal Horse Artillery," " Royal Welch Fusiliers.")

(BOB *goes cheerfully, if a trifle unsteadily, out of the french windows.* ETHEL *crosses below the table and up* C., *and locks the windows. She turns and regards* FRANK *thoughtfully for a moment. He is above the* R. *end of the table.*)

FRANK (*holding up his hand*). Bite it back. You'll only regret it.

ETHEL. The next time you go to a regimental dinner you can go to a hotel afterwards and sleep it off. I won't have it, d'you hear? This is my dining-room, this is, not a bar parlour!

FRANK. I wish it was.

ETHEL. Go on, get up to bed and don't make a noise either —— (*She turns and catches sight of* QUEENIE'S *note on the mantelpiece.*) What's that?

FRANK. What's what?

ETHEL (*going to it*). This letter.

FRANK. I haven't written no letters.

ETHEL (*taking it*). It's Queenie's writing—— (*She opens it.*)

FRANK. Here—you can't read the girl's private letters.

ETHEL (*grimly*). It's addressed to you and me.

FRANK. Well I'll be damned! (*He comes to* C., *above the table.*)

(ETHEL *reads the letter through and then stands quite still, staring out front.* FRANK *goes over to her. She hands it to him.*)

ETHEL. She's gone. Read it. (*She sits down quietly in the armchair above the fire and buries her face in her hands.*)

FRANK (*reads the letter carefully*). Who's this man? Have you ever seen him?

ETHEL. No.

FRANK. I'll fetch her back—I'll give her the hiding of her life.

ETHEL. You can't find her. She doesn't say where she's gone.

FRANK (*reading*). "—we love each other—his wife won't divorce him—we can't live without each other so we are going away." (*He crumples the letter in his hand.*) It's our own fault. (*He breaks a little down* R. *and turns.*) We might have known something like this would happen—we let her have her own way too much, ever since she was a child—Queenie—— (*His voice breaks.*)

(ETHEL *sits quite still without saying anything.* FRANK *goes to her,* R. *of the armchair.*)

We'll trace her all right—don't you worry. We can find out who the man is through the shop. It must have been there she met him. We'll get her back.

ETHEL (*with sudden violence*). I don't want her back ! She's no child of mine. I don't want ever to see her again as long as I live.

FRANK. Don't say that, Ethel. (*He breaks a little towards* C., *and turns.*)

ETHEL (*controlling herself*). I mean it. I've done my best to bring her up to behave respectable, to be a good girl, but it hasn't been any use.

FRANK (*by the chair at the* L. *end of the table*). If she loves this man all that much—maybe it was too strong for her—maybe she couldn't help herself——

ETHEL (*looking at him*). You don't see what she's done the same way as I do—do you ?

FRANK. I don't know.

ETHEL. You and me never have quite seen eye to eye about what's right and what's wrong. You'd have her back to-morrow if she'd come, wouldn't you ? But I wouldn't. You've always encouraged her and told her how clever she was, and let her twist you round her little finger——

FRANK. All I've done is to try laughing at her instead of scolding her.

ETHEL. Well, you've got something to laugh at now, haven't you ?

FRANK (*a pace nearer to* ETHEL). Don't go for me, Ethel—she's my girl as well as yours.

ETHEL. I'm not going for anybody. I've done my best. I can't do more.

FRANK. You can't stop loving the girl all at once, even if she has done wrong.

ETHEL. I can try.

FRANK. What's the sense of that ?

ETHEL. It isn't anything to do with sense—it's how you feel.

FRANK. I've never seen you like this before. You're hard as nails, aren't you ?

ETHEL. What d'you expect me to be ?

FRANK. I don't know—I suppose you never cared for Queenie as much as you did the other two.

ETHEL. It's not fair to say that.

FRANK (*breaking a pace down and to* R.). It's true though, isn't it ? (*He half sits on the* L. *end of the table, staring down.*)

ETHEL. No, it is not. She's always been the most trouble, that's true enough, and she's certainly never put herself out to try and help me like Vi has ; that's true too, but I've cared for her just as much as the others, and don't you start saying I haven't. It's no use trying to lay the blame for this at my door. What she's done she's done on her own, and I'll never forgive her for it until the end of my days.

FRANK (*crossing to the fire*). If you feel like that it's not much good talking about it, is it ? (*He stands by the lower end of the mantelpiece, with his back to* ETHEL.)

ETHEL (*after a pause—rising*). Will you turn out or shall I ?

FRANK (*turning pleadingly*). Ethel——

ETHEL (*stonily*). I'm going back to bed now. (*She turns and crosses above the table.*) You might put those things back in the sideboard before you come up.

She goes down to the door and out, without looking at him. When she has gone FRANK *puts* QUEENIE'S *letter in his pocket, goes wearily over to the table and puts the biscuits, O.K. sauce and bloater-paste into the cupboard. He sits down above the table for a minute and finally buries his head in his arms as—*

The lights fade and the CURTAIN *falls.*

SCENE 3

TIME.—*May, 1932. It is about four-thirty on a fine afternoon. The french windows are wide open. Out of sight in the garden* FRANK *is weeding.*

MRS. FLINT *is knitting in her chair by the fireplace.* SYLVIA *is at the table with a newspaper and a dictionary, doing a crossword puzzle. A brand-new shining radio stands on the whatnot at back,* R. *of the window. It is playing softly.* EDIE *comes in and out with the tea-things.*

SYLVIA (*with satisfaction, scribbling*). Got it !

MRS. FLINT. What ?

SYLVIA. A biblical name in five letters with an " s," in the middle—Moses.

MRS. FLINT. I could have thought of that.

SYLVIA. Pity you didn't then. I asked you just now.

MRS. FLINT. Why's tea being laid so early ?

SYLVIA. Because Frank's taking us to the Majestic.

MRS. FLINT. I wish somebody'd turn that radio off—it's getting on my nerves.

SYLVIA (*rising and going up* R.C.). Ethel'd have it playing all day just because Reg gave it to her—— (*She turns the radio off.*)

MRS. FLINT. Well, the skies'll fall next, I shouldn't wonder, you doing something I asked you without grumbling.

SYLVIA (*returning to above the* L. *end of the table*). Now then, Mrs. Flint, don't start.

MRS. FLINT. I wasn't starting anything, just passing a remark.

SYLVIA (*folding up the paper*). Well, I've done that now all except the long one across and the short one down with an " x " in it.

MRS. FLINT. I must say, having a steady job at the library's done you a world of good.

SYLVIA (*taking the paper to the little table down* L.). I don't know what you're talking about.

MRS. FLINT. You're not so touchy as you used to be—flying off at the least thing.

SYLVIA (*primly*). I'm very glad, I'm sure.

MRS. FLINT. It was a lucky day for all of us when you met that Mrs. Wilmot.

SYLVIA (*returning up* L.C.). I don't know to what you're referring.

MRS. FLINT. Oh yes, you do.

SYLVIA (*turning to* MRS. FLINT). I wish you'd stop going at me about everything for once. (*She picks up her dictionary.*)

MRS. FLINT. I was only saying it was a good thing you meeting that Mrs. Wilmot.

SYLVIA (*going to the sideboard with the dictionary*). Well, we won't argue about it, will we ?

MRS. FLINT. You haven't had one of your headaches for weeks, have you ?

SYLVIA (*sharply*). No, I have not.

MRS. FLINT. There you are, then.

SYLVIA (*returning slowly to* C., *above the table*). Perhaps you'd rather have me the way I was before—not sleeping a wink at night and suffering and being in error.

MRS. FLINT. In what ?

SYLVIA. Error !

MRS. FLINT. Oh, so that's what it was.

SYLVIA. And you needn't sneer at Mrs. Wilmot either—she's a wonderful woman.

MRS. FLINT. She must be, to make you believe there wasn't anything the matter with you. It's what I've been saying for years.

(SYLVIA *turns* R., *adjusting the tea-things on the table.*)

SYLVIA (*brightly*). Well, then, we won't say anything more about it, will we ?

MRS. FLINT. We will if we feel like it.

(FRANK *comes in from the garden. He is in his shirt-sleeves.*)

FRANK. How long before tea's ready ? (*He moves a little down* L.C.)

EDIE (*entering with the milk and sugar*). About five minutes—the kettle's on.

FRANK. Tell Ethel to start without me, Sylvia—I've got one more bed to do. Where is she ?

SYLVIA. Upstairs, lying down.

FRANK (*catching sight of a vase on the mantelpiece*). Who put that may in here ?

SYLVIA. I did—it's such a pretty colour.

(FRANK *crosses to the mantel.*)

FRANK (*taking it out of the vase*). You ought to know better than to bring may into the house.

SYLVIA. Why ever not ?

FRANK (*returning to* L.C.). It's unlucky.

SYLVIA (*with a great display of amusement*). Why, Frank, really ! What a thing to believe——

FRANK. You was born in the country the same as I was, Sylvia—it's a long while ago, I'll admit. . . .

SYLVIA (*tossing her head*). There's no need to be nasty—you and your old may——

FRANK (*going out again*). Well, don't do it again.

SYLVIA (*moving down* R. *of the table—bus. with the tea-things*). Frank's been a changed man since Queenie went.

MRS. FLINT. I haven't noticed much difference.

SYLVIA. Do you think she'll ever come back ?

MRS. FLINT. She'll get a piece of my mind if she does. Bringing disgrace on all of us.

SYLVIA (*below the table to the* L. *end*). Frank had a letter from her the other day.

MRS. FLINT (*looking at her, sharply*). How d'you know ?

SYLVIA (*moving up between the table and the armchair*). It came by the midday post along with that letter I had from Mrs. Wilmot —Edie was upstairs doing the front room and I took it in myself. I recognized the handwriting——

MRS. FLINT. Think he told Ethel ?

SYLVIA (*breaking a little* R., *above the table*). Not very likely—she doesn't let him mention her name if she can help it. (*She sits in the chair above the table.*) It had a French stamp.

MRS. FLINT. Disgusting !

ETHEL (*coming in* P). What's disgusting ?

MRS. FLINT. Gracious, Ethel, what a start you gave me !

ETHEL (*down* R.).   What was disgusting ?

SYLVIA.   A French stamp.

ETHEL.   French stamp ?   What are you talking about ?
(*She closes the door.*)

SYLVIA.   We were talking about the letter Frank had from
Queenie.

ETHEL (*going to the* R. *end of the table*).   Oh, were you ?

MRS. FLINT.   Then it *was* from Queenie ?

SYLVIA.   You knew about it ?

ETHEL.   It's a pity that Christian Science of yours hasn't
taught you to mind your own business among other things,
Sylvia.

SYLVIA.   Well, I'm sure I don't see what I've done !

ETHEL.   You know perfectly well I won't 'ave Queenie's name
spoken in this house.   She's gone her own way and that's that.
She doesn't belong here any more.

MRS. FLINT (*with relish*).   I always knew that girl would come
to no good.

(SYLVIA *rises and turns a little up* C.)

ETHEL.   Once and for all, will you hold your tongue, Mother !
I'm sick to death of you and Sylvia gabbing and whispering
behind my back.

(SYLVIA *turns to face down stage.*)

MRS. FLINT.   Well, I like that, I must say——

ETHEL.   I don't care whether you like it or not—be quiet.
Where's Frank ?

SYLVIA (*sullenly*).   In the garden—he's started on another bed.

ETHEL.   Tea's just ready.

SYLVIA (*returning to behind her chair at the table*).   He said we
were to begin without him.

(EDIE *comes in with the teapot.*   ETHEL *sits down at the* R. *end of
the table and begins to pour out.   There is a silence.*   EDIE *goes
out again.*)

(*To* MRS. FLINT.)   Are you coming to the table or shall I bring
it over to you ?

MRS. FLINT.   I'll stay here—the less I open my mouth the
better.

ETHEL (*giving* SYLVIA *a cup of tea*).   Here, Syl, take it over to
her.

SYLVIA (*bringing the tea to* MRS. FLINT).   Bread and
butter ?

MRS. FLINT.   No, thank you.   (*As* SYLVIA *turns to go.*)   I'll
'ave a petit beurre if there is one.

SYLVIA.   All right.

(*She takes the biscuits from the table to* MRS. FLINT. MRS. FLINT *takes some, and* SYLVIA *returns to the table and sits down. There is another silence.* ETHEL *gets up and turns on the radio again.*)

ETHEL (*returning to the* R. *end of the table*).   Sorry I flew out at you like that, Sylvia.

SYLVIA (*gracefully*).   It doesn't matter, I'm sure.

ETHEL (*sitting again*).   I dropped off to sleep on my bed this afternoon and had a bad dream.

SYLVIA.   What was it ?

ETHEL.   I can't remember—I woke up feeling as if the world had come to an end.

SYLVIA (*cheerfully*).   Well, they say dreams go by contraries.

ETHEL.   Yes, they do, don't they ?

MRS. FLINT.   These teeth of mine are getting worse and worse —I can't bite a thing.

ETHEL.   Try soaking 'em.

MRS. FLINT.   I am.

ETHEL.   I wish Frank'd come in to his tea—we shall be late next thing we know.

SYLVIA.   Why not take a cup out to him ?   He never eats much anyhow.

ETHEL (*glancing at the clock*).   It's nearly half-past now.

SYLVIA.   I'll take it if you like.

ETHEL.   No, I will.   Once he starts weeding he'd go on all night if we let him.

(*She pours out a cup of tea and goes out into the garden with it.*)

SYLVIA.   You'd better be going upstairs to put your hat on, hadn't you ?

MRS. FLINT.   Lots of time.   Frank'll have to wash before he goes.

(*There is a ring at the front-door bell.*)

SYLVIA.   Now I wonder who that is ?

MRS. FLINT.   It might be Reg and Phyl.

SYLVIA.   Can't be—they've gone to Sevenoaks with them friends of theirs.

MRS. FLINT (*listening*).   Has Edie gone ?

SYLVIA.   Yes—I heard her come out of the kitchen.

(*The door opens and* VI *comes quickly into the room. She looks pale and she is trembling.*)

Why, Vi ?   (*Rising.*)   Whatever's the matter ?

VI (*closing the door*).   Where are Mum and Dad ?   (*She comes to above the chair* R. *of the table.*)

SYLVIA.   In the garden.

VI (*hurriedly*).   Take Granny upstairs—there's been an accident—it's Reg and Phyl—I've got to tell Mum and Dad.

MRS. FLINT. What's that ? (*She puts her cup on the work-basket* L. *of her chair.*)

SYLVIA. What sort of an accident ? What happened ?

VI. They were in Reg's car and a lorry came out of a turning——

SYLVIA. Are they badly hurt ?

VI. They're dead.

SYLVIA. Oh my God ! (*She sinks back into her chair above the table.*)

VI. Mrs. Goulding was with them, she knew I had a telephone and so she rung me up from the hospital. She was in the back and got thrown out—please take Granny upstairs—I must tell them alone.

SYLVIA (*bursting into tears*). Oh my God ! Oh my God !—— (*She rises, then buries her face in her hands.*)

VI (*going to her*). Don't cry, Auntie Sylvia—they'll hear you —don't let them hear you. (*She glances up at the windows.*)

SYLVIA (*sobbing*). I can't believe it—I can't——

VI (*to* SYLVIA). Auntie Sylvia—please—— (*She moves up* R.C., *and checks, looking at the windows.*)

SYLVIA *crosses* L.C., *with a great effort at control but still sobbing, and helps* MRS. FLINT *across, moving* R., *below the table. When* SYLVIA *and* MRS. FLINT *have gone,* VI *closes her eyes for a minute, braces herself and goes out into the garden. The room is empty for a minute or two, and there is no sound except for the radio playing softly and the mowing machine next door. Presently* FRANK *and* ETHEL *come in alone. His arm is round her and they neither of them speak. He brings her slowly to the chair by the fireplace and puts her gently down into it. Then he draws up the chair* L. *of the table and sits next to her. He reaches out for her hand and they sit there in silence as—*

The lights fade and the CURTAIN *falls.*

ACT III

Scene 1

TIME.—*December the 10th, 1936.*

It is just after ten o'clock in the evening. The remains of supper have been pushed aside to make way for the radio, which is standing in the middle of the table.

Round it are sitting FRANK, ETHEL *and* SYLVIA. FRANK *sits below the table* R. ETHEL *above it and* SYLVIA L. *of it.* VI *is in the chair above the fire,* SAM *in the chair below it.*

King Edward the Eighth's farewell broadcast after his abdication has just finished. SYLVIA *is in tears. Everyone else is silent.*

FRANK and ETHEL *have aged a good deal in the four years since* REG'S *death. They are only fifty-two and fifty-one respectively, nevertheless they look older.* SYLVIA, *on the other hand, who is after all the same age as* ETHEL, *looks, if anything, a little younger than before. This is doubtless attributable to the assurance acquired from Christian Science and the brisk example of Mrs. Wilmot.* VI *and* SAM *appear to be the settled, comfortable married couple that they are.* SAM, *indeed, having put on weight, seems definitely middle-aged.*

As the CURTAIN *rises, and the lighting fades in, the radio makes a few discordant wheezes and groans.* FRANK *rises and turns it off.*

FRANK. Well—that's that. (*He crosses* L.) Funny to think that that's being listened to all over the world. (*He takes a cigarette from the mantelpiece.*) There won't be anything more to listen to to-night, all the stations have closed down. (*This last phrase as he crosses to* R., *and exits.*)

(*There is silence for a moment, broken only by* SYLVIA'S *sniffs.* ETHEL *rises, crosses to the calendar on the wall below the fire, takes it down, and drops it into the wastepaper basket down* L.)

SYLVIA (*who has turned to see this*). Ethel—what are you doing ?

ETHEL (*crossing* R. *to the door*). It's near the end of the year anyhow.

(*She exits.*)

VI (*rising*). Better put the radio back where it belongs. Give me a hand, Sam——

(SAM *rises, and together they move the radio back to the whatnot up* R.)

SAM (*during the above bus.*). We'll have to be going in a minute. Mrs. Burgess said she couldn't stay after half-past ten and we can't leave the children in the house all by themselves.

(SYLVIA *rises and begins to pack up the supper things.*)

VI (*moving down* R.). I'll pop up and get me hat—I left it in Mum's room.

(*She exits.*)

SAM (*crossing back to the fireplace*). How's the library going, Aunt Sylvia ?

SYLVIA (*clearing the table*). All right—but I'm leaving it next month.

SAM (*standing* L., *with his back to the fire*). I thought you liked working there.

SYLVIA (*getting a tray from below the sideboard*). Oh, it's not bad, but I'm going in with Mrs. Wilmot. She wants me to assist her in her reading and rest room in Baker Street.

SAM. Oh, I see.

SYLVIA. How are the children ?

SAM. Sheila's all right, but Joan's been a bit seedy the last few days.

SYLVIA (*brightly*). Poor little thing.

SAM. The doctor said she never quite got over that cold she had in November.

SYLVIA (*indulgently—crossing to the sideboard with the sugar-basin*). Did he indeed ?

SAM (*slightly nettled*). Yes, he did. She was running a bit of a temperature a couple of nights ago, so we've kept her in bed ever since.

SYLVIA (*returning to the table to fold the cloth*). I suppose if you believe in doctors, it's best to do what they say.

SAM. Well, it stands to reason they know a bit more about it than we do, doesn't it ?

SYLVIA. No, I don't think it does !

SAM (*incensed*). What would you do if you broke your leg ? I suppose you'd send for a doctor then, wouldn't you ?

SYLVIA (*going to the sideboard and putting the cloth in the upper drawer*). I wouldn't break my leg.

SAM (*pressing*). But if you *did* ? If you were run over through no fault of your own——

SYLVIA (*going down to the door*). I should certainly send for treatment.

SAM. There you are then !

SYLVIA (*with a pitying smile, opening the door*). You don't understand, Sam. (*She goes to the table, picking up the tray.*)

After all, there isn't any reason why you should. (*She goes to the door.*) You haven't studied the matter, have you ?

(*She exits.*)

SAM (*raising his voice slightly*). No, I haven't.

SYLVIA (*re-entering and pushing in the chair at the table* R.). It wouldn't be surgical treatment I should send for. It would be spiritual treatment.

SAM. Would that heal a compound fracture ?

SYLVIA. Certainly. (*She goes below the table.*)

SAM. Before I'd believe that I'd have to see it with my own eyes.

SYLVIA (*pushing in the chair below the table*). If you believed first, you wouldn't have to worry whether you saw it with your own eyes or not.

SAM. Oh, yes, I should.

SYLVIA (*with sweet, unassailable superiority, pushing in the chair* L. *of the table*). Dear Sam !

(FRANK *re-enters* R.)

FRANK. Where's Ethel ?

SYLVIA (*above the table*). In the kitchen, I think. (*She puts the chair up* L. *of the whatnot.*)

FRANK (*crossing towards* L.). We miss Edie and that's a fact. (*Up* L.C.) I've tried to make her get someone else, but she won't.

SYLVIA (*pushing in the other chair above the table, then going to the sideboard*). There's not so much to do since Mrs. Flint passed on.

FRANK (*facing* R.). I do wish you wouldn't talk like that, Sylvia, it sounds so soft.

SYLVIA (*brings down the centre doily*). I don't know what you mean, I'm sure.

FRANK (*firmly*). Mother died, see ! First of all she got 'flu and that turned to pneumonia and the strain of that affected her heart, which was none too strong at the best of times, and she *died*. Nothing to do with passing on at all.

SYLVIA. How do you know ? (*Putting the fern from the sideboard on the centre of the table.*)

FRANK. I admit it's only your new way of talking, but it gets me down, see ?

(ETHEL *comes in again, followed by* VI *in her hat and coat.*)

ETHEL (R. *of the table*). What are you shouting about ?

FRANK (R. *of the armchair above the fire*). I'm not shouting about anything at all. I'm merely explaining to Sylvia that Mother died. She didn't pass on or pass over or pass out—she *died* !

VI (*down* R., *giggling*). Oh, Dad, you do make me laugh, really you do!

ETHEL. It's not a fit subject to talk about, anyhow.

VI. Come on, Sam—we must be going. Good night, Mother. (*Kissing* ETHEL.)

ETHEL. Good night, dear. If you want to go out to-morrow afternoon I'll come and look after the children.

VI. Thanks a lot. Good night, Dad.

FRANK. So long, Vi.

VI. Good night, Auntie Sylvia. Don't pay any attention to Dad. He's an old tease.

(*She exits* R.)

SAM (*closing the door*). Good night, all.

FRANK (*crossing* R.). I'll come to the door with you.—Where's Archie, Ethel?

ETHEL. Asleep in the kitchen. He's been out once to-night

(SAM *and* FRANK *exit* R.)

SYLVIA (*above the* L. *end of the table*). I think I'll go up to bed now, Ethel.

ETHEL (*above the table*). All right, dear.

SYLVIA. What about the washing-up?

ETHEL. I'll do the lot to-morrow morning. I've left everything in the sink for to-night.

SYLVIA (*dutifully kissing her*). Then good night.

ETHEL. Good night.

(SYLVIA *goes down* L. *of the table and crosses* R.)

SYLVIA (*sighing as she goes out*). Oh, dear!

(ETHEL *crosses* L., *glances at the clock, and then, taking some socks out of a work-basket on the table by the fireplace, sits down in the armchair and begins to darn.* FRANK *re-enters* R.)

FRANK. Vi's looking a bit peaky, isn't she? (*He closes the door.*)

ETHEL. She's worried about Joan, I think.

FRANK (*crossing to the fire*). She'll be all right—remember the trouble we had with Queenie when she was tiny?

ETHEL (*coldly*). Yes, I do.

FRANK. Sorry—I forgot.

ETHEL. You're lucky.

(FRANK *turns at the fireplace to look down at her.*)

FRANK (*sadly*). You are a funny woman, Ethel, and no mistake.

ETHEL. I expect I am. We're as God made us, I suppose, and there's nothing to be done about it.

FRANK. Well, all I can say is He might have done a better job on some people without straining Himself.

ETHEL. How often have I told you I won't 'ave you talking like that, Frank.

FRANK. I wasn't meaning you.

ETHEL. I don't care who you was meaning. If you don't believe in anything yourself, you can at least have the decency to spare the feelings of them as do.

FRANK. As a matter of fact, I believe in a whole lot of things.

ETHEL. Well, that's nice to know.

FRANK. One of 'em is that being bitter about anybody isn't a good thing, let alone if it happens to be your own daughter.

ETHEL. I'm not bitter. I just don't think of her any more, that's all.

FRANK. That's one of the things I don't believe.

ETHEL. Don't let's talk about it, shall we ?

(*A pause.*)

FRANK (*crossing slowly to above the table* R.C.). I wish you'd have another girl in place of Edie. (*He turns and sits on the edge of the table.*)

ETHEL. I don't need one now there's only the three of us. Sylvia helps every now and again and the char does the heavy cleaning once a week.

FRANK. We could afford it quite easily.

ETHEL. Maybe we could—but getting a strange girl used to our ways would be more trouble than it was worth.

FRANK. What anybody ever wanted to marry Edie for beats me.

ETHEL. No reason why they shouldn't. She was a good girl and a good worker.

FRANK. Exactly the reasons I married you.

ETHEL. Don't talk so silly.

FRANK (*rising and breaking a little* L.C.). She may not be much to look at—I said to myself—but there's a worker if ever I saw one !

ETHEL. Haven't you got anything better to do than to stand there making funny remarks ?

FRANK. There's nothing much I want to do.

ETHEL. Why don't you have a nice read of the paper ?

(*There is a tap on the window.*)

That'll be Bob. Now I can get on with me darning.

(FRANK *goes up to the window, opens it and admits* BILLY. BILLY *is now thirty-four and wearing the uniform of a Warrant Officer. He has grown a little more solid with the years, but apart from this there is not much change in him.*)

FRANK (*backing a pace down, R. of the window*). Well, here's a surprise ! Billy !

BILLY. Hallo, Mr. Gibbons.

(*He goes to* ETHEL L., *who has risen at* L.C. FRANK *closes the windows.*)

ETHEL. Why, Billy—I'd no idea you was back. (*She shakes hands.*)

BILLY (*breaking to C.*). I've got a couple of weeks' leave. I've been transferred from a cruiser to a destroyer.

(ETHEL *sits again.*)

FRANK (*moving down L.C.*). D'you like that ? (*He crosses to the fire.*)

BILLY. You bet I do.

FRANK (*with his back to the fire*). What's the difference ?

BILLY. Oh, lots of little things. To start with, I live in the wardroom—then I keep watches when we're at sea—and well, it's sort of more friendly, if you know what I mean.

FRANK. Like a drink ?

BILLY. No, thanks. I just had one with Dad.

ETHEL. Is he coming in ?

BILLY. Yes, I think so—a bit later on.

ETHEL. He must be glad you're back. It must be lonely for him in that house all by himself since your mother was taken.

FRANK. Nora *died*, Ethel ! Nobody took her.

(BILLY *takes out his cigarette-case.*)

ETHEL. You ought to be ashamed, talking like that in front of Billy.

BILLY (*lights a cigarette*). It was a blessed release really, you know, Mrs. Gibbons, what with one thing and another. She'd been bedridden so long——

ETHEL. Would you like me to go and make you a cup of tea ? It won't take a minute.

BILLY. No, thanks, Mrs. Gibbons—there's something I want to talk to you about as a matter of fact—both of you.

FRANK. All right, son—what is it ?

BILLY. I feel a bit awkward really—I wanted Dad to come with me and back me up, but he wouldn't.

FRANK. A man of your age hanging on to his father's coat-tails, I never 'eard of such a thing. What have you been up to ?

ETHEL (*putting down her work, with sudden premonition, sharply*). What is it, Billy ?

BILLY. It's about Queenie.

(*There is silence for a moment.* ETHEL *puts her work aside.*)

ETHEL (*hardening*). What about her ?

BILLY. Does it still make you angry—even to hear her name !
ETHEL. I'm not angry.
FRANK. Have you seen her, Billy ?
BILLY. Yes—I've seen her.
FRANK (*eagerly*). How is she ?
BILLY. Fine.

(*There is another silence.* BILLY *turns a little up* L.C., *and then back to* C.)

ETHEL (*with an obvious effort*). What is it that you wanted to say about Queenie, Billy ?
BILLY (*in a rush ; breaking to her a little*). I sympathize with how you feel, Mrs. Gibbons—really I do—and what's more she does too. She knows what a wrong she did you in going off like that. It didn't take her long to realize it. She hasn't had any too good a time, you know. In fact, she's been through a good deal. (*He breaks above the table.*) He left her—the man she went off with—Major Blunt—after about a year. He went back to his wife. He left Queenie stranded in a sort of boarding-house in Brussels.
ETHEL (*bitterly*). How soon was it before she found another man to take her on ? (*She takes up her darning.*)
FRANK. Ethel !
BILLY. A long time—over three years.
ETHEL (*bending over her darning*). She's all right now then, isn't she ?
BILLY. Yes—she's all right now.
FRANK (*crosses to below the* L. *end of the table*). What sort of a bad time did she have—how d'you mean ?
BILLY. Trying to earn a living for herself—getting in and out of different jobs. (*He turns and goes down* R. *of the table to* R.C.) She showed dresses off in a dressmaker's shop for over a year, I believe. By that time she had a little money saved and was coming home to England to try and get her old mani-curing job back when she got ill with appendicitis and was taken to hospital——
FRANK. Where—where was she taken to hospital ? How long ago ? (*He sits at the* L. *end of the table.*)
BILLY. Paris—about a year ago. (*Moving across to the fire.*) Then, when she was in the hospital, she picked up with an old Scotswoman who was in the next bed and a little while later the two of them started an old English tea-room in Mentone in the south of France—you know, just for the English visitors. That's where I ran into her by accident. We were doing a summer cruise and the ship I was in laid off there. A couple of pals and I went ashore to have a cup of tea—and there she was !

(FRANK *is staring towards* R.)

ETHEL. Is she there now ?

BILLY. No, she isn't there now.

FRANK *(turning in his chair to face* L.*).* Where is she, then ?

BILLY. She's here.

(FRANK *rises.*)

ETHEL. Here !

FRANK. How d'you mean—here ?

BILLY. Next door—with Dad.

ETHEL *(rising to her feet and dropping her darning on the floor).*
Billy !

BILLY. We were married last week in a registry office in
Plymouth.

ETHEL. Married !

BILLY *(simply).* I've always loved her, you know—I always
said I'd wait for her.

FRANK *(brokenly).* Oh, son—*(crossing to* BILLY) I can't
believe it.—Oh, son !

(*He wrings* BILLY's *hand wildly and then almost runs out through
the french windows.* BILLY *breaks to* L.C., *and turns to* ETHEL.)

BILLY. You'll forgive her now, won't you, Mrs. Gibbons ?

ETHEL *(in a strained voice).* I don't seem to have any choice,
do I ?

BILLY. I always thought you'd like to have me for a son——

ETHEL. Better late than never !—that's what it is, isn't it ?—
(*She starts half laughing and crying at the same time.*)—Better late
than—never— Oh dear ! . . .

(BILLY *helps her to sit again.*)

BILLY. Shall I get you a little nip of something ?

ETHEL *(tearfully).* Yes, please——

BILLY. Where is it ?

ETHEL. In the sideboard cupboard.

(BILLY *goes quickly to the sideboard, takes a bottle of whisky out
and pours some, neat, into a glass. He brings it to her. He
gives her the glass, crossing below her to the* L. *of her chair, and
she sips a little. He takes her left hand and pats it affectionately.*
FRANK *comes back through the window leading* QUEENIE *by the
hand. She is soberly dressed and looks pale. There is a strained
silence for a moment.* FRANK *is* R. *of* QUEENIE. ETHEL *rises.*)

QUEENIE. Hallo, Mum.

ETHEL. So you've come back, have you—you bad girl.

QUEENIE *(coming slowly across the room to her).* Yes, Mum.

ETHEL *(putting her arms round her).* A nice way to behave,
I must say—upsetting me like this——

The lights fade and the CURTAIN *falls.*

Scene 2

Time.—*September 30th, 1938.*
It is about nine o'clock in the evening.

Ethel *and* Queenie *have finished their supper and gone upstairs to see if* Queenie's *four-months-old son is sleeping all right.* Sylvia *and* Vi *are still at the table.* Sylvia *sits* L. *of the table.* Vi *is above it.*

Sylvia. Is there any more hot water in the jug ?
Vi. No—there isn't.
Sylvia. I thought I'd like another cup.
Vi (*jumping up*). I'll run and get some.
Sylvia (*not moving*). Don't worry, dear—I'll go.
Vi. You stay where you are, Auntie Syl—it won't take a minute.

(*She runs out with the jug.* Sylvia, *left alone, sits pensively with her chin resting on her hands. In a moment or two,* Vi *returns with the hot water.*)

Sylvia (*as she comes in*). I always knew it, you know.
Vi. Always knew what ?
Sylvia. That there wouldn't be a war.

(Vi *puts the jug on the table,* R. *of* Sylvia.)

Vi. Well, I thought there would, I must say, otherwise I shouldn't have sent Sheila and Joan down to Mrs. Marsh in Dorset.

(Sylvia *pours water into the teapot.*)

Sylvia. I know you did, dear. Your mother was worried too about Queenie and little Frankie—but I wasn't. Neither was Mrs. Wilmot.
Vi. Fancy that now. (*Crossing to the mantel for a cigarette.*)
Sylvia (*turning in her chair*). Mrs. Wilmot laughed outright, you know, when the woman came to try on her gas-mask. "Take that stupid thing away," she said. Just like that—quite simply. The woman was furious. (*She pours herself a cup of tea.*)
Vi (*lighting her cigarette*). I'm not surprised.
Sylvia. It's funny how cross people get when you refuse to believe in evil. (*She sips her tea.*)
Vi. It's rather difficult not to believe in evil, Auntie Syl, when you think of what's going on in different parts of the world just now.
Sylvia. If enough people believed in good, none of it would happen.

Vi. Yes, but they don't, do they ?

Sylvia (*turning again in her chair*). You remind me of your father sometimes, Vi ; you're material-minded.

Vi. Well, I can't help that, can I ?

Sylvia. Well, if you don't mind me saying so—I think you can.

Vi (*sitting on the chair below the fire*). As far as I can see, facts are facts, Auntie Syl, and if looking at it like that means I'm material-minded, I'm afraid that's what I shall go on being.

Sylvia. You don't understand what I mean, dear.

Vi. No—I'm afraid I don't.

Sylvia. To begin with, what you call facts may not be facts at all.

Vi. What are they then ?

Sylvia. Illusion—and error.

Vi. Isn't error a fact then ?

Sylvia (*a little rattled*). Of course it is in a way—that's just the trouble. But still, if you admit it's a fact and regard it as a fact, it makes it more of a fact than ever, doesn't it ?

Vi. I shouldn't think it made much difference one way or the other.

Sylvia. But it *does* !

Vi. You mean that when Sheila had toothache the other day I ought to have told her that she hadn't.

Sylvia. I don't mean any such thing.

Vi. What do you mean then ?

Sylvia. I mean that if she had been brought up to believe that pain is evil and that evil doesn't really exist at all, she wouldn't have had toothache in the first place.

Vi. But she'd broken it on a bit of toffee and the nerve was exposed.

Sylvia. Nonsense. (*She turns back to her tea.*)

Vi (*rising*). It isn't nonsense, Auntie Syl—it's true.

Sylvia. I wish Mrs. Wilmot was here.

Vi. I'm sure I'm glad she isn't.

Sylvia. It shows a very small mind to talk like that, Vi—you ought to be ashamed. Mrs. Wilmot is a very remarkable woman.

Vi. She sounds a bit silly to me.

Sylvia (*rising*). We will not discuss the matter any further. (*She goes above the table and begins to clear.*)

Vi. All right.

Sylvia. Your very life has been saved at this moment by the triumph of right thinking over wrong thinking.

Vi (*equably*). Well, that's nice, isn't it ?

Sylvia. I've often thought Mr. Chamberlain must be a Christian Scientist at heart.

VI. Well, let's hope that Hitler and Mussolini are too, and then we shall all be on velvet.

(FRANK *comes in wearing his hat and coat.*)

FRANK. What are you two looking so glum about ?

VI. We were talking about Mr. Chamberlain. Auntie Syl says she thinks he must be a Christian Scientist.

FRANK (*going out again*). That might account for a lot.

SYLVIA. What did you want to say that for, Vi—you're a very aggravating girl.

VI. Sorry.

SYLVIA. Just because you haven't any faith in anything yourself, you think it's funny to laugh at people who have. (*She continues to pack up the supper things.*)

VI. I wasn't laughing at all.

FRANK (*re-entering, having taken off his hat and coat*). Where's your mother ?

VI. Upstairs with Queenie and his lordship.

FRANK (*crossing* L., *to below the armchair*). Nothing wrong with him, is there ?

VI (*below, and to* L. *of* FRANK). Oh, no—he's fine. Queenie's not feeling any too good, so she went to bed—her leg was hurting her a bit. It's nothing serious, the doctor came this afternoon to have a look at her, and said it was only brought on by the strain of the last week——

FRANK. I'll go up in a minute.

SYLVIA. Did you see anything of the crowds ?

FRANK (*laconically*). Yes, I did.

VI (*sitting in the chair below the fire*). We heard him arrive at the airport, on the radio.

FRANK. So did I.

VI. Sam's meeting me at the Strand Corner House a little later on. We thought we'd have a look at the West End. It ought to be exciting.

FRANK. Well, it's exciting all right, if you like to see a lot of people yelling themselves hoarse without the faintest idea what they're yelling about.

SYLVIA (*up* R.C.). How can you, Frank ! They're cheering because we've been saved from war.

FRANK. I'll cheer about that when it's proved to me.

SYLVIA (*hotly, moving to above the* L. *end of the table*). You wouldn't care if there was another war. You're one of those people that think it doesn't matter that millions and millions of innocent people should be bombed !—Just because you enjoyed yourself in the last one——

FRANK (*firmly, moving to* L. *of* SYLVIA). Now listen here, Sylvia. Don't you talk to me like that because I won't 'ave it—see ? I did *not* enjoy myself in the last war—nobody but a bloody fool without any imagination would ever say that he did.

(SYLVIA *sits*.)

And I do not think it doesn't matter if millions and millions of innocent people are bombed! So you can get them silly ideas out of your head to start with. But what I would like to say is this. I've seen something to-day that I wouldn't 'ave believed could happen in this country. I've seen thousands of people, English people, mark you! carrying on like maniacs, shouting and cheering with relief, for no other reason but that they'd been thoroughly frightened, and it made me sick and that's a fact! And I only hope to God that we shall have guts enough to learn one lesson from this and that we shall never find ourselves in a position again when we have to appease anybody! (*He breaks to the fire.*)

SYLVIA. All you men think about is having Guts and being Top Dog and killing each other, (*rising*) but I'm a woman and I don't care how much we appease as long as we don't have a war.

(FRANK *turns to face her*.)

War is wicked and evil and vile—They that live by the sword shall die by the sword—It's more blessed to give than to receive——

FRANK. I don't think it's more blessed to give in and receive a nice kick on the bottom for doing it.

ETHEL (*coming in*). Will you two stop shouting—you'll wake up Frankie! (*She moves to above the* R. *end of the table*.)

SYLVIA. He's a warmonger, that's all he is—a warmonger!

FRANK. Judging by the 'eavy way you're breathing, Sylvia, I should say you was in error!

SYLVIA (*bursting into tears of rage*). You're no brother of mine—I don't want to speak to you ever again——

(*She rushes out of the room and slams the door, crossing below the table*.)

ETHEL (*putting the biscuit-barrel in the sideboard*). What's the use of arguing with her, Frank? You know it never does any good.

VI (*rising*). She started it, Mother. (*Crossing* R. *to above the table*.) She was ever so silly. She's getting sillier and sillier every day.

ETHEL. Don't you talk about your Aunt Sylvia like that.

VI (*kissing her*). Dear old Mum, I'm thirty-five you know now, not fifteen.

ETHEL (*putting the cruet in the sideboard*). All the more reason for you to know better.

VI. There you are, you see! (*Turning to look at* FRANK.) Mum'll never learn.

Ethel. I don't care if you're a hundred and five, I won't have you being saucy to your Aunt Sylvia, or to me either for that matter.

Vi (*breaking to* L.C.). What about Dad ? I can be saucy to him, can't I ?

Ethel. Get on with you, Miss Sharp !

Vi. I'm just going, anyhow—I'm picking up Sam—we're going to see the crowds. (*She laughs at* Frank.) Sorry, Dad——

Frank. You can cheer your head off for all I care. Why don't you take a squeaker with you ?

Vi (*crossing down* L. *of the table to* R.). Maybe I will—I'll just pop up and see Queenie for a minute. Good night, all——

Frank. Good night. (*He moves to the downstage end of the fire.*)

Ethel (*crossing* L.). Don't forget to send round that pram.

Vi (*turning at the door*). Sam'll bring it to-morrow.

(*She exits.*)

Ethel (*sitting down in the armchair above the fire*). What a week ! I wouldn't have believed I could be so tired.

Frank (*looking down at* Ethel). Yes—you look a bit done up. How's Queenie ?

Ethel. She's all right. You'd think nobody'd ever had a baby before ! All the fuss we've had the last month.

Frank (*crossing slowly to up* L.C.). She got up too soon.

Ethel. She had a letter from Billy this afternoon. He wants her to go out there.

Frank (*turning*). She can't yet, she's not strong enough.

Ethel. He didn't say yet—he said after Christmas—all being well.

Frank. The baby won't be old enough to travel.

Ethel. She'll leave him here.

Frank. With us ?

Ethel. Of course—don't be so silly—who else would she leave it with !

Frank (*sitting on the* R. *arm of* Ethel's *chair*). That'll be fine, won't it ?

Ethel. Fine for you maybe—you won't 'ave to look after it.

Frank. Perhaps you'd rather she left it with Vi ! Or put it in a nice clean home of some sort.

Ethel. Don't be a bigger fool than you can help—go on upstairs and say good night to her before she drops off

(Frank *kisses* Ethel.)

That's enough.

Frank (*rising and crossing down* R., *to the door*). I'm expecting Bob to come in and have a farewell binge—give me a shout when he comes.

ETHEL. Binge indeed! One small one's all you're going to have, my lad, if I have to come down and take the bottle away from you.

FRANK (*cheerfully—going out*). I'd like to see you try.

(*Left alone, ETHEL gets up and goes over to the sideboard cupboard. She takes out the whisky bottle and a syphon. She has just done this when BOB taps at the window. She goes up C., and lets him in.*)

BOB. Hallo, Ethel. (*He moves down L.C.*)

ETHEL. Frank's just saying good night to Queenie—he'll be down in a minute. (*She fastens the windows and then crosses above the table to the sideboard.*)

BOB. What a week! What with the crisis and the sandbags and me having to pack up all the furniture into the bargain.

ETHEL. Has most of it gone? (*She brings the whisky, etc., to the table.*)

BOB. Yes—went this afternoon. I'm sleeping on a camp-bed to-night.

ETHEL. Frank'll miss you.—So shall I.

BOB. I'm not going very far—you'll both come down and see me, won't you?

ETHEL (*clearing the table*). Of course we will, Bob. I've often wondered why you stayed on so long in that house all by yourself.

BOB. Oh, I don't know. It was near you and Frank—and it was somewhere for Billy to come home to.

ETHEL. You'll feel a bit lost, I expect—living in the country.

BOB. Well, I shall have me garden—a damn sight nicer one than I've got here—and there's the sea nearby—and the village pub!

ETHEL. We'll come down and see you quite soon—(*moving to below the table*)—I'll go and tell Frank you're here.

BOB. Righto. (*There is a slight pause.*) Good-bye, Ethel.

ETHEL (*uncertainly*). Good-bye, Bob. (*She goes to him and kisses him.*) Take care of yourself.

(*She turns and goes swiftly out of the room.*)

(*Off stage.*) Bob's here.

FRANK (*off*). Rightho.

(*After a moment FRANK comes in.*)

FRANK (*crossing below the table*). Well, he's back. Umbrella and all!

BOB. Yes.

FRANK (*round to above the table*). Let's have a drink. I'm feeling a bit low—what with one thing and another. (*He starts to pour out the drinks, above the R. end of the table.*) Only one good thing's happened.

BOB (*crossing to* L. *of* FRANK). What's that ?

FRANK. If Queenie goes out to Singapore after Christmas, we're taking charge of the kid.

BOB. I thought you'd get him. (*He takes his glass from* FRANK.)

FRANK. Well, you couldn't have had him—all alone by the sad sea waves.

BOB. All right, all right, no hard feelings.

FRANK (*holding up his glass*). Here goes.

BOB (*doing the same*). Happy days !

FRANK. Remember the first night we moved in ? When we had Sylvia's Wincarnis ? (*He moves round* R. *of the table to below it.*)

BOB. That's going back a bit.

FRANK. Nearly twenty years.

BOB. And here we are—just the same.

FRANK. Are we ?

BOB (*with a sigh, sitting at the* L. *end of the table*). No—I suppose we're not.

FRANK. It's a strange world. (*Sitting in the chair below the table.*) All them years—all the things that happened in 'em—I wouldn't go back over them for all the rice in China—would you ?

BOB. Not on your life.

FRANK. Remember that picnic we 'ad at Box Hill in nineteen-twenty-three and you got tiddley, and fell down and sprained your ankle ?

BOB. Whatever made you think of that ?

FRANK. I don't know, I was just thinking——

BOB. Remember that summer holiday—the one we all had together—before Nora got ill ?

FRANK. The year we went to Bognor ?

BOB. That's right.

FRANK. That must have been earlier still—let's see, Reg was fourteen—that would have been nineteen-twenty-two——

BOB. I remember you and Ethel having a row about going out in a boat.

FRANK. Yes—— (*He laughs.*) Ethel's always hated going out in a boat.

BOB. I remember the night we went to your regimental dinner too—the night Queenie went off——

FRANK. Reg was still alive then, wasn't he ?

BOB. Yes—that was about a year before.

FRANK (*looking round*). I wonder what 'appens to rooms when people give 'em up—go away and leave the house empty——

BOB. How d'you mean ?

FRANK. I don't know. I was just thinking about you going away from next door after all that time and me and Ethel going away too pretty soon. I shouldn't think we'd stay on here much longer—and wondering what the next people that live in this room will be like, whether—they'll feel any bits of us left about the place——

BOB. 'Ere, shut up! You're giving me the willies!

FRANK (*rising*). Have another spot? (*He reaches for the whisky and syphon.*)

BOB. Just a small one.

FRANK. Funny you going to live just near where I was born.

BOB. It's about eleven miles, isn't it?

FRANK. Less than that if you go by the marsh road, but it takes longer. I'll probably come back there one day, I hope—that is if I can get round Ethel. She hates the country.

BOB. I suppose it's all according to what you're used to.

FRANK (*handing him his drink*). You don't think the Germans will ever get here, do you?

BOB. No—of course I don't.

FRANK (*sitting on the lower edge of the table*). I'm feeling a bit bad about all this business.

BOB. I'm not feeling too good myself.

FRANK. I'm going to miss you a hell of a lot.

BOB. Same here—you'll be coming down though, won't you?

FRANK. You bet.

BOB (*lifting his glass*). Here's to you, old pal.

FRANK (*doing the same*). Here's to you, old pal.

The lights fade and the CURTAIN *falls.*

SCENE 3

TIME.—*June, 1939.*

It is a warm summer evening and the french windows are wide open. It is still daylight and, as in Act I, Scene 1, the may tree is in bloom at the end of the garden. Also as in Act I, Scene 1, the room is almost empty of furniture. The pictures have been taken down from the walls and the curtains from the windows. There is a muddle of packing-cases, luggage, parcels, shavings, paper and string. The mantelpiece is denuded of ornaments, but the armchair is still by the fireplace, and the sideboard, looking strangely bare, is still in its accustomed place, although jutting out from the wall a trifle, as if it were afraid of being left behind.

From upstairs comes the sound of intermittent hammering.

VI *comes in from the garden wheeling a pram. She wheels it carefully through the window and brings it to a standstill to lean against the crate down* R.C. *She gives a look to see if its occupant is all right, and then goes to the door.*

VI (*calling*). Mum . . .

ETHEL (*off stage*). Yes, dear?

Vi. I'll have to be getting along now.

Ethel. All right, dear.

Vi. I've brought him in.

(Ethel *appears. She looks a little flustered and untidy.*)

Ethel. Has he been good ? (*She moves round below the pram, and sits on the crate above it.*)

Vi. Good as gold. I gave him the postcard Queenie sent with the camel on it—he liked it.

Ethel (*looking into the pram*). He's dropped off now.

Vi (*crossing below the pram to* L.C., *and turns*). There's nothing more I can do to help, is there ?

Ethel. No, thanks, dear—everything's done now. They're coming for the rest of the stuff in the morning. I'm just getting a bit of supper for your dad and me in the kitchen—we're going to walk round to the flat afterwards.

(Vi *stands behind* Ethel *and massages her neck as she sits on the crate* c.)

Vi. I do hope you'll like it, Mum.

Ethel. Well, it's got a nice view of the Common, I will say that for it.

Vi. You'll find it easier being on one floor, of course.

Ethel. Yes—I suppose I will.

Vi. It looked quite nice to me—a bit modernistic, of course.

Ethel. Well, that can't be helped.

(*More hammering is heard upstairs.*)

Vi. It'll be a comfort, anyway, having running hot water instead of having to fuss about with a geyser.

Ethel. One thing less for your dad to grumble about.

Vi (*moving to the pram for her bag—listening*). He's enjoying himself with that hammer, isn't he ? (*She breaks towards the door.*)

Ethel (*rising and moving to the pram*). The more noise the better's his motto.

Vi (*calling*). Dad . . .

Frank (*upstairs*). Hello . . .

Vi (*opening the door*). I'm going now.

Frank. Righto—see you in the morning.

Vi (*going to* Ethel). Good night, Mum.

Ethel (*kissing her absently*). Good night, dear.

Vi. I'll bring Archie round to-morrow when I come. The children'll miss him.

Ethel. I don't see why you don't keep him really, you know. After all, you've got a little garden, which is more than we'll have in the new flat.

Vi. Oh, Mum—what'll Dad say ?

ETHEL. He won't mind much. (*Crossing to the chair above the fire.*) Poor old Percy was his choice, you know. He never took to Archie in the same way.

VI. Thanks ever so much, Mum—if you feel after a time you want him back, all you've got to do is just say.

ETHEL. All right, dear.

VI. Well—so long. (*She moves up* C.)

ETHEL. Thank you for coming, dear—give my love to Sam and the children.

VI. I will. (*Turning at the windows.*) Good night.

ETHEL. Good night . . .

(VI *exits to the garden.* ETHEL *sits in the armchair and closes her eyes.* FRANK *comes downstairs and into the room. He is in his shirt-sleeves and carries a hammer.*)

FRANK. Hello—having a breather ?

ETHEL. I am that. My back's breaking.

FRANK (*putting the hammer down on the sideboard*). Not as young as you were.

ETHEL. Who are you to talk ?

FRANK. How's his lordship ? (*He looks into the pram.*)

ETHEL. Don't wake him up now.

FRANK. He's dribbling—dirty boy.

ETHEL. I expect you dribbled when you was his age.

FRANK. I do still, as a matter of fact, if I happen to drop off in the afternoon.

ETHEL. Well, it's nothing to boast about.

FRANK (*moving to* R. *of* ETHEL's *chair*). Bit snappy, aren't we ?

ETHEL. Who wouldn't be with all I've had to do to-day !

FRANK (*bending over her and giving her a kiss*). Poor old crock.

ETHEL. Leave off, Frank—we haven't got time for fooling about.

FRANK (*taking off his armbands*). That's just where you're wrong. We've got all the time in the world.

ETHEL. All right—have it your own way.

FRANK (*moving up to the windows*). I shall miss that garden.

ETHEL. Well, it's your own fault—you're the one that wanted to move.

FRANK. I know.

ETHEL. You'll have the balcony, anyhow. You can put window-boxes all round it.

FRANK (*coming down a little*). Window boxes ? One day—a bit later on—when I stop working, we might get a little place in the country, mightn't we ?

ETHEL. And when will that be, may I ask ?

FRANK. Oh, I don't know. In a few years, I suppose

ETHEL. Well, we'll think about that when the time comes.

FRANK. I think you'd like the country, you know, Ethel, once you got used to it.

ETHEL. That's as may be.

FRANK. I know you're frightened of it being a bit too quiet for you, but when people get old they don't mind so much about being quiet.

ETHEL. We're not all that old yet, you know.

FRANK. We ought to go abroad some day, by rights.

ETHEL. Whatever for ?

FRANK. Well, I feel a bit silly sometimes, having been working over other people's journeys for twenty years and never so much as set foot out of England meself since nineteen-nineteen.

ETHEL. Well, if you want to go gadding about to foreign parts you'll have to do it by yourself . . .

FRANK. What a chance ! (*Moving round to below the crate* C.). You'd be after me like an electric hare.

ETHEL. You flatter yourself.

FRANK (*pensively*). It's a funny thing . . .

ETHEL. What is ?

FRANK. You'd think taking all the furniture out of a room would make it look bigger, but this one looks smaller. (*To above the crate, looking around.*)

ETHEL (*with a touch of vehemence*). I shall be glad when we're out of it.

FRANK (*breaking to* R. *of the crate*). So shall I—sorry, too, though, in a way.

ETHEL (*rising*). Well, I've rested long enough—I must go and get on with the supper . . .

(*She crosses to him below the crate. He quite quietly puts his arms round her. She submits and rests her head on his shoulder. They stand there together in silence for a moment.*)

FRANK. It's been a long time all right.

ETHEL. Yes.

FRANK (*gently*). I don't mind how many flats we move into or where we go or what we do, as long as I've got you . . .

ETHEL (*in a low voice*). Don't talk so silly . . .

(*She disentangles herself from his arms and goes quickly out of the room with her head down. FRANK looks after her for a moment, smiling, then saunters over to the pram. He stands looking down into it for a little.*)

FRANK. Hello, cock !—So you've decided to wake up, 'ave you ? Feel like a bit of upsie-downsie ? Well, Frankie-boy, I wonder what you're going to turn out like ! . . . There's nobody here to interrupt us, (*he gets out his cigarettes*) so we can talk as man to man, can't we ? . . . There's not much to worry about really, so long as you remember one or two things always. The first thing is that life isn't all jam for anybody, and you've got to have trouble of some kind or another, whoever you are. But if you don't let it get you down, however bad it is, you won't go far wrong . . . (*He lights a cigarette.*) Another thing you'd better get into that little bullet head of yours is that you belong to something that nobody can't ever break, however much they try. And they'll try all right—they're trying now. Not only people in other countries who want to do us in because they're sick of us ruling the roost—and you can't blame them at that !—but people here, in England. People who have let 'emselves get soft and afraid. People who go on a lot about peace and good will and the ideals they believe in, but somehow don't seem to believe in 'em enough to think they're worth fighting for. (*He sits on the crate.*) The trouble with the world is, Frankie, that there are too many ideals and too little horse sense. We're human beings, we are—all of us—and that's what people are liable to forget. Human beings don't like peace and good will and everybody loving everybody else. However much they may think they do, they don't really because they're not made like that. Human beings like eating and drinking and loving and hating. They also like showing off, grabbing all they can, fighting for their rights and bossing anybody who'll give 'em half a chance. You belong to a race that's been bossy for years and the reason it's held on as long as it has is that nine times out of ten it's behaved decently and treated people right. Just lately, I'll admit, we've been giving at the knees a bit and letting people down who trusted us and allowing noisy little men to bully us with a lot of guns and bombs and aeroplanes. But don't worry— that won't last—— The people themselves, the ordinary people like you and me, know something better than all the fussy old politicians put together. We know what we belong to, where we come from, and where we're going. We may not know it with our brains, but we know it with our roots. And we know another thing too, and it's this. We 'aven't lived and died and struggled all these hundreds of years to get decency and justice and freedom for ourselves without being prepared to fight fifty wars if need be—to keep 'em !

(ETHEL *enters* R.)

ETHEL. What in the world are you doing ? Talking to yourself ?

FRANK. I wasn't talking to myself—I was talking to Frankie.

ETHEL. Well, I'm sure I hope he enjoyed it.

FRANK. He's stopped dribbling, anyhow !

ETHEL. Come on in—supper's ready—you'd better close the windows, he might get a chill.

(*She turns* R. *and exits.* FRANK *closes the windows and goes back to the pram.*)

FRANK. So long, son . . .

He goes out as—

The CURTAIN *falls.*

FURNITURE AND PROPERTY PLOT

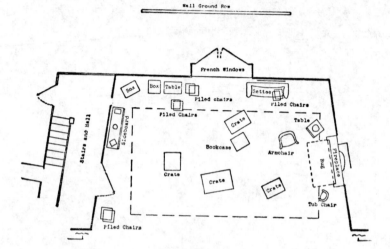

ACT I

SCENE 1

June, 1919. 8.30 *p.m. Night*

Curtains *open* and tied.
Windows *open*.
May *in bloom*.
Packing-cases as on plan.
Door *closed*.
Brackets *off*.
Fire *off*.
Sideboard R.
Aspidistra.

In the Sideboard.—Jam.
  Whisky.
  Syphon.
  Paste.
  O.K. sauce.

In the Drawer R.—2 knives.
  Runner.

In the Drawer L.—Green cloth.

In the Case R.C.—Biscuit-barrel.
  Metal fern.
  Clock.
  Tobacco-jar.
  Blue metal vase.

92

Green vase.
Metal vase.
Metal and glass ornament.
Metal stool.
Small vase.
Small pot.

In the Hearth.—Kettle.
Fender.
Fireirons.
Trivet.

On the Mantel.—Cigarettes and matches.

Off R.—Penknife.
Hammer.
Tacks.
Bottle of Wincarnis.
2 glasses.
Carrier of provisions with can of beans and pepper tints.

PERSONAL.
Handkerchief (FRANK).

EFFECTS.
Hammering.

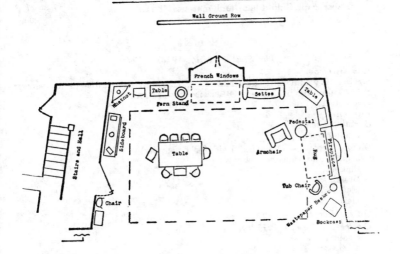

SCENE 2

Christmas Day, 1925. 3.0 *p.m. Afternoon.*

Windows and door *shut.*
Curtains *open.*
Ivy on pictures.
May is *green.*
9 chairs round the table (1 R. and 1 L., 4 above and 3 below : 2 of these
    are bedroom chairs).
Fire *on.*
Brackets *off.*

On the Table R.C.—Laid for 9.
  Fruit in green dish.
  Nut-crackers.
  Box of crackers.
  Preserved fruit.
  Glasses.
  Bottles of wine.
  Pie.
  Cake.
  2 red candles.
On the Pedestal.—Workbasket (MRS. FLINT).
On the Sideboard.—Whisky.
  Syphon.
  4 glasses.
  Crackers.
  Fern in silver holder.
Waste basket above the sideboard.
On the Bamboo Table.—Bullrushes.
On the Shelves.—Aspidistra and leaves.
On the Whatnot.—Large pot with fern.
PERSONAL.
  Off R.—Large tray (EDIE).
  Paper cap, Gold Flake and matches (FRANK).

SCENE 3

The Strike. May, 1926. *Night.*

May *in bloom.*
Strike : Ivy and Christmas effects. Strike fern from table to whatnot.
Set : Tulips on bookcase. Otherwise flowers remain.
Brackets *on.*
Fire *on.*
Curtains *open.*
Windows *open.*
On the Table C.—(5 chairs) Laid for 6 (supper)
  3 cups and saucers down R.
  Cheese.
  Bread.
  Hot water.
  Ham.
On the Bookcase.—Tulips.
On the Sideboard.—Whisky.
  Syphon.
  4 glasses.
  Cruet.
  Fern (remains).
On the Bamboo Table.—Bag and cigarettes (QUEENIE).
PERSONAL.
  Off R.—Bowl of soup (VI).
  Slice of toast on plate (QUEENIE).

ACT II

Scene 1

The Wedding.   October, 1931.   10 o'clock.   Morning.

Curtains *open.*
Windows *shut.*
May is *green.*
Strike : Tulips, bullrushes and glass down L.
  Aspidistra from the window to the sideboard and leaves from the
  window to the bamboo table.

On the Sideboard.—Aspidistra.
  Whisky.
  4 glasses.
  Ashtray.
  Syphon.
In the Drawer.—Green cloth.
On the Pedestal.—Workbasket (MRS. FLINT).
On the Shelves.—Chrysanthemums.
On the Table C. (4 chairs).—Laid for one (breakfast).
  Toast.
  Milk-jug.
  Teapot.
  Hot water.
  Egg, plate and spoon.
  " Daily Mirror."
  Bread-board, bread and knife.
  Marmalade.
On the Mantel.—Gold Flake.
  Matches.
  Bag (QUEENIE).
On the Bamboo Table.—Hat-box.
  Pot of leaves.
  Beneath it.—Workbasket.
On the Whatnot.—Green fruit-dish.
PERSONAL.
  Off R.—Tray (EDIE).
  Upstairs.—2 ties (REG).

Scene 2

Drunk Scene.   November, 1931.   Midnight.

Strike : Tie from the mantel.
  Chrysanthemums from the shelves.
  Tea-things from the sideboard.
  Leaves from the bamboo table to the shelves and aspidistra from the
    sideboard to the shelves ; replace with bullrushes and ferns.
Curtains *closed.*
Windows *shut.*
Door *open.*
On the Sideboard.—Whisky and syphon.
  4 glasses.
  Fern.
In the Sideboard.—2 knives.

Inside.—O.K. sauce.
  Fish paste.
  Biscuits in barrel.
On the Table R.C. (4 chairs).—Fruit in green dish.
  Ashtray.
On the Whatnot.—Fern.
On the Shelves.—Leaves and aspidistra.
On the Bamboo Table.—Bullrushes.
NOTE.—*No chair below the table.*

SCENE 3
Death.   May, 1932.   Afternoon.

May *in bloom.*
Curtains *open.*
Windows *open.*
The flowers remain.
Strike : Green fruit dish from centre of the table and fern from the
  whatnot.
On the Table R.C.—Tea laid for 5 (4 chairs).
  Biscuits (Petit Beurre).
  Bread and butter.
  Dictionary, pencil and newspaper (SYLVIA).
On the Whatnot.—Radio.
On the Mantel.—May.
Off R.—*Tray :* Milk and sugar.
  Tray : Teapot with rubber spout.
    Cosy.
    Hot water.
EFFECTS.
  Radio.
  Door-bell.

ACT III
SCENE 1

Abdication.   December, 1936.   10 p.m.   Night.

Strike : Bullrushes and set the vase of chrysanthemums.
  Picture and set mirror.
  Dictionary.
Set : Green fruit dish on the sideboard.
Flowers remain. (Shelves remain.   Fern on the sideboard.)
Curtains *closed.*
Windows *shut.*
Fire *on.*
Brackets *on.*
Change : Curtains.
  Armchair above the fire.
  New covers for the settee and chairs.
On the Table R.C.—Red cloth.
  Half-white cloth.
  5 cups, saucers and spoons.
  Teapot and green cosy.
  Milk.
  Sugar.
  Hot water.

On the Sideboard.—Green fruit dish.
  Fern.
Beside the Sideboard (R.).—Tray.
On the Flat down L.—Calender.
  Beneath it.—Waste-basket.
On the Bamboo Table.—Chrysanthemums in the vase.

PERSONAL.
  Cigarettes and matches (BILLY).

SCENE 2

Munich. September, 1938. Evening.

May *is green.*
Strike : Calender from waste-basket.
  Glass down L.
  Vase of chrysanthemums.
  Aspidistra from shelves and leaves ; replace with geraniums.
Set : Roses on the bookcase.
In the Sideboard.—Whisky and syphon.
  2 glasses.
On the Table R.C.—Supper for 4.
  Cruet.
  Magazine.
  Teapot with cosy.
  Milk, sugar, hot water.
  Biscuit-barrel.
  Pickles.
  (Set nothing down stage on table.)
On the Bamboo Table.—Aspidistra.
Off R.—Hot water.

SCENE 3

Moving Out. June, 1939. Evening.

Windows *open.*
Strike : Everything but the settee and the bamboo table, the sideboard
  4 single chairs, armchair above the fire ; armchair below the fire
  goes to up stage R., with rug in it.
Introduce 5 packing-cases and 2 suitcases.

Off R.—Pram.

EFFECTS.
  Hammering.

LIGHTING PLOT

EQUIPMENT USED

Bracket upstage of fireplace, L.
Bracket downstage of fireplace, L.
Bracket upstage of door, R.
Bracket on backing off stage, R.
Fire and fire spot, L.
Door bell set.
2 *Lengths :* 1 upstage and 1 downstage of door, R.
2 *Floods :* 1 L. and 1 R. on ground row.
2 *Floods :* 1 L. and 1 R. on backcloth.
Panatrope, with speaker up stage L.

SPOT CHART

No. 5.—36 pink on table and sideboard (C. and up R.).
No. 9.—52 gold on windows (up C.).
No. 12.—36 pink on chair below the fireplace (down L.).
No. 13.—36 pink on chair above the fireplace (up L.).
No. 15.—36 pink on packing-case C.
No. 16.—36 pink directed as No. 15.

ACT I

SCENE 1

To Open.—Black Out.
On Cue.—Fade in all spots.
 Floats and No. 1 batten : No. 4 amber and No. 3 straw—FULL.
 Nos. 4 and 5 battens : No. 4 amber, No. 3 straw and open white—FULL.
 Floods on ground row : No. 3 straw.
 Floods on backcloth : No. 17 blue.
 Amber lengths on interior backings.
On Cue.—*As* BOB *and* FRANK *drink*—Fade to Black Out.

SCENE 2

To Open.—Black Out.
On Cue.—Fade in all spots—FULL.
 Floats and No. 1 batten—FULL.
 No. 5 batten : No. 4 amber—FULL.
 Fire and fire spots.
 Amber lengths on interior backings.
Cue 1.—*On entrance of* BILLY—Slow fade in amber in No. 5 batten to ½
 Follow with No. 1 batten to ½, floats ½, and all spots *except* Nos. 12 and 13
 Fire, and fire spots, and door lengths not changed.
 (NOTE.—This check should take 4½ minutes.)
Cue 2.—ETHEL. " Getting quite dark, isn't it ? "—A pause, then fade
 out to Black Out.

SCENE 3

To Open.—Black Out.
On Cue.—Fade in all spots—FULL.
 No. 1 batten and floats—FULL.

98

2 floods on backcloth (18 blue and 3 straw).
Fire and fire spot.
Brackets.
Door lengths.

Cue 1.—*As* FRANK *switches off at door down* R.—Snap out of everything
except door lengths and fire and fire spot.

ACT II
SCENE 1

To Open.—Black Out.
On Cue.—Fade in as Act I, Scene 1.
Cue 1.—*On*—FRANK. " Come on, old girl . . ."—Fade to Black Out

SCENE 2

To Open.—Fire and fire spot and door lengths ON.
Cue 1.—*As* QUEENIE *switches* ON *at the door down* R.—Snap in all spots—
FULL.
No. 1 batten and floats—FULL.
Brackets.

Cue 2.—*As* QUEENIE *switches* OFF—Snap out.
Cue 3.—*As* BOB *switches* ON—Snap on.
Cue 4.—*As* FRANK *buries his head in his arms*—Fade everything to
Black Out.

SCENE 3

To Open.—Black Out.
On Cue.—Fade in as Act I, Scene 1.
Cue 1.—FRANK *sits by* ETHEL, *and reaches for her hand*—A pause, then
fade to Black Out.

ACT III
SCENE 1

To Open.—Black Out.
On Cue.—Fade in all spots—FULL.
No. 1 batten and floats—FULL.
Brackets.
Fire and fire spot.
Door lengths.

On Cue.—ETHEL. " . . . upsetting me like this . . ."—Then fade to
Black Out.

SCENE 2

To Open.—Black Out.
On Cue.—Fade in as Act I, Scene 3.
Cue 1.—FRANK. " Here's to you, old pal . . ."—They drink as fade to
Black Out.

SCENE 3

To Open.—Black Out.
On Cue.—Fade in as Act I, Scene 1.

No fade out at CURTAIN.

AGE TABLE

SCENES	ACT I 1	2	3	ACT II 1	2	3	ACT III 1	2	3
Frank	35	41	42	47	47	48	52	54	55
Ethel	34	40	41	46	46	47	51	53	54
Sylvia	34	40	41	46	46	47	51	53	54
Bob	37	43	44	49	49	50	54	56	—
Mrs. Flint	60	66	67	72	72	73	—	—	—
Vi	—	20	21	26	—	27	31	33	34
Queenie	—	19	20	25	25	—	30	—	—
Reg	—	18	19	24	—	—	—	—	—
Billy	—	21	—	27	—	—	32	—	—
Phyllis	—	18	19	24	—	—	—	—	—
Sam	—	19	20	25	—	—	30	—	—
Edie	—	25	26	31	—	32	—	—	—